Music Games, Brain Teasers and Puzzles

By Lynne Davis

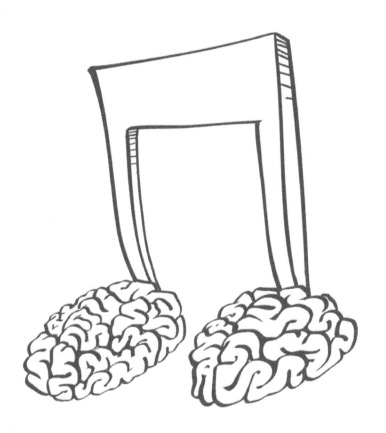

The author wishes to acknowledge the inspiration of many other educators in creating the contents of this book, including Joe Hubbard and Sandy Bourgeois. Each of the pages in this volume is available individually in reproducible digital format at lynnedavis.com.

ISBN978-1-7337419-0-3

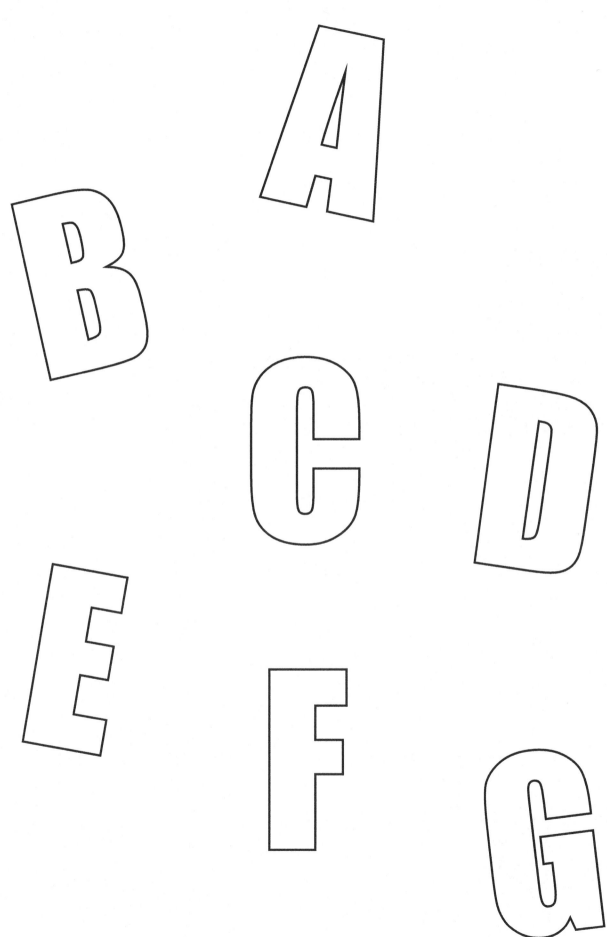

Color the treble clef RED.

Color the bass clef BLUE.

Color the repeat sign GREEN.

Color the flat symbol PINK.

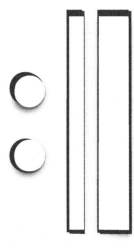

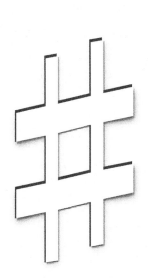

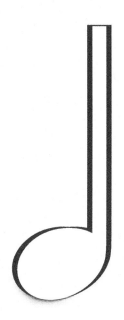

Color the sharp symbol ORANGE.

Color the quarter note BLACK.

Color the eighth notes PURPLE.

Color the natural symbol YELLOW.

Color the forte symbol ORANGE.

Color the fermata symbol BROWN.

Color the piano symbol LIGHT BLUE.

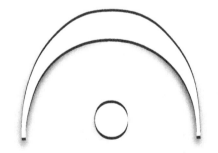

Color the time signature RED.

Color the eighth note PURPLE.

Color the slur LIGHT GREEN.

Color the staccato note PINK.

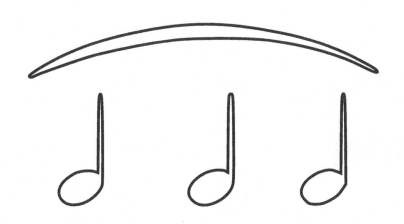

Rainbow Piano

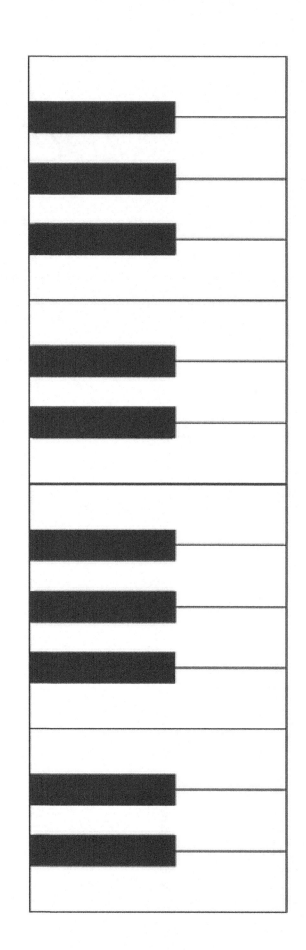

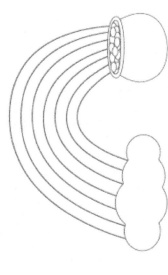

Color all the C's RED.

Color all the D's YELLOW.

Color all the E's LIGHT BLUE.

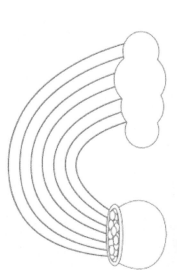

FINGER NUMBERS

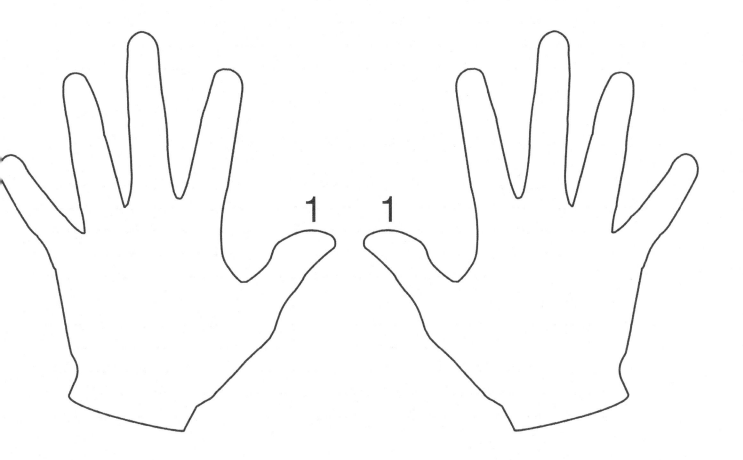

1   1

Place finger numbers on each hand.
Then color in the hands.

LINES and Spaces of the Staff

The music staff has 5 lines and 4 spaces.

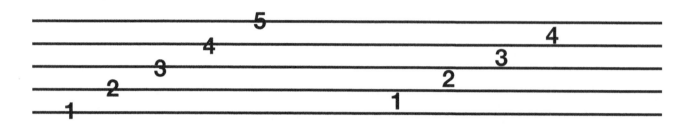

Copy the numbers of the lines and spaces on the staves below.

Write the letters of the music alphabet, beginning from each letter. Time yourself reading the entire page. Then time yourself doing the entire page **from memory!**

My Time: _____

A						

B						

C						

D						

E						

F						

G						

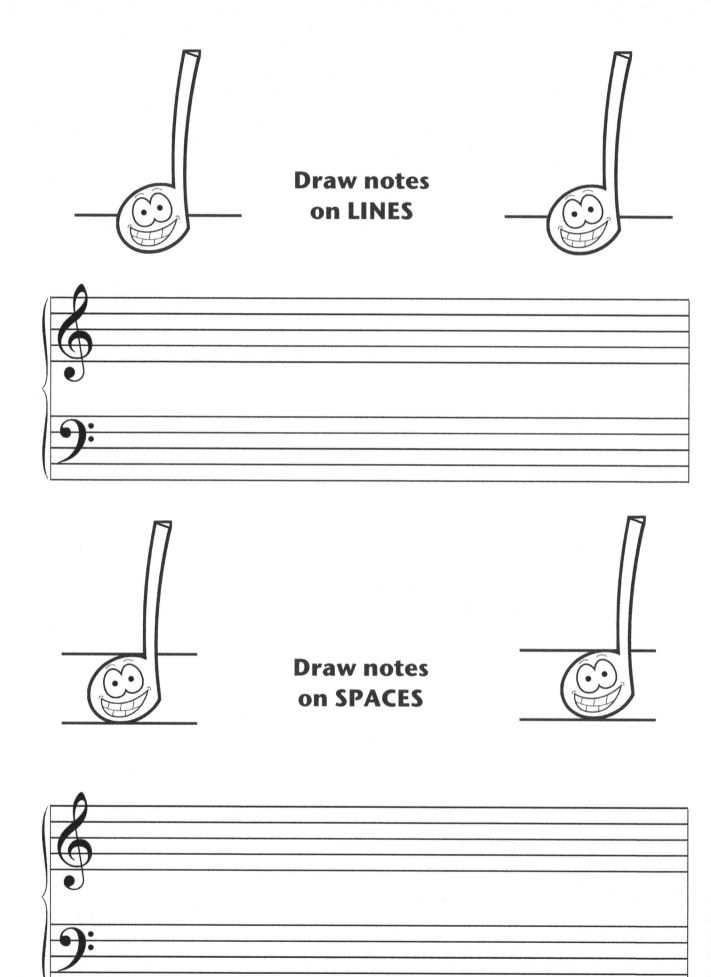

Draw notes on LINES

Draw notes on SPACES

Draw notes that are STEPPING

line - space - line - space

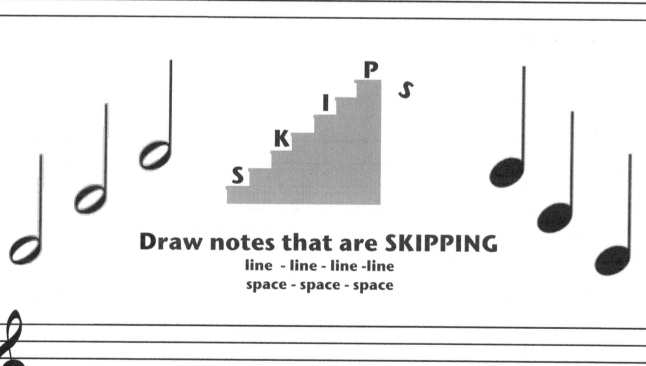

Draw notes that are SKIPPING

line - line - line -line
space - space - space

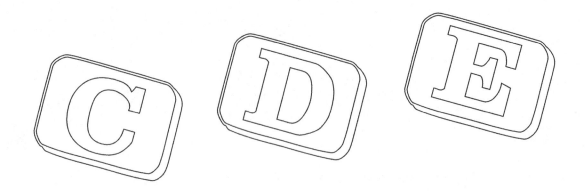

Draw the notes, C, D and E on the **treble clef** staff.

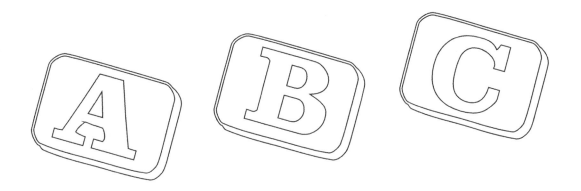

Draw the notes, A, B and C on the **bass clef** staff.

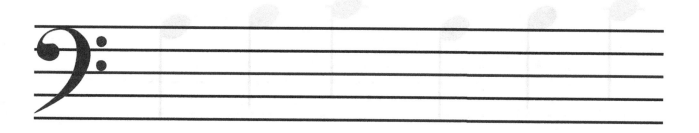

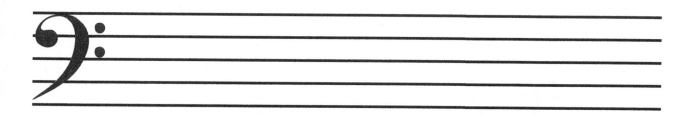

Draw the notes in the C position on the **grand staff**.

Notes in the C Position

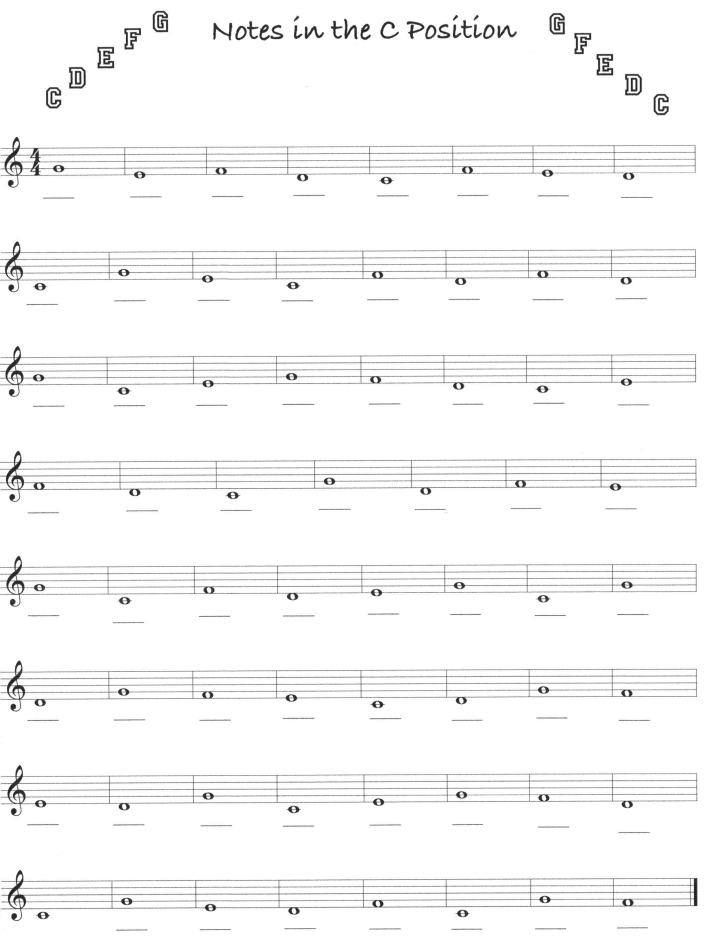

15

Draw the notes in the G position on the **grand staff**.

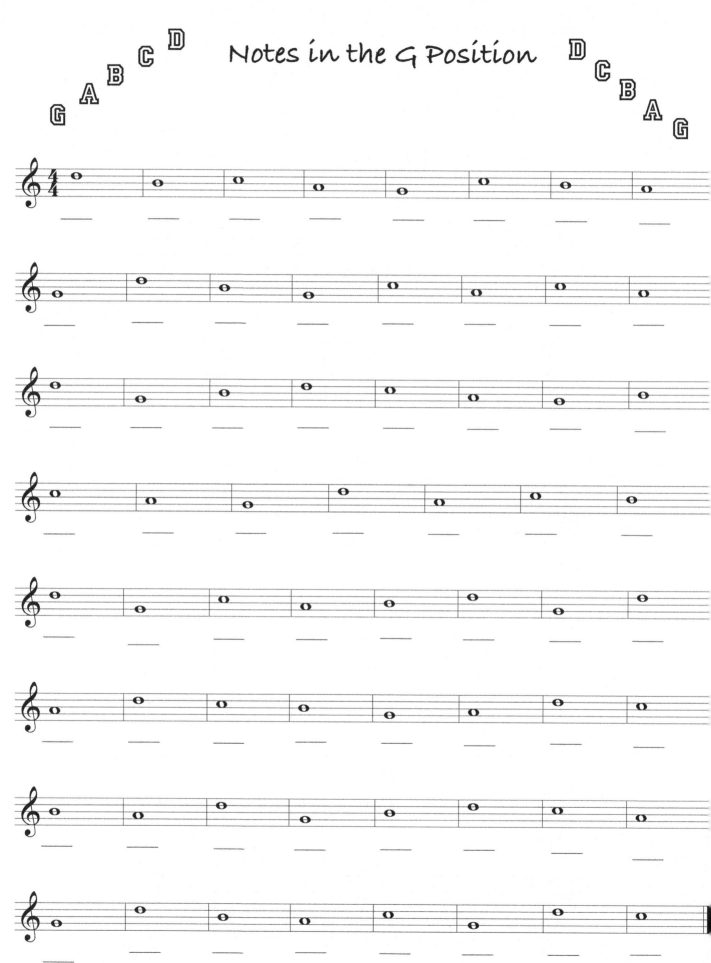

Notes in the G position

MUSIC SYMBOLS MATCHING

Match the symbols to their names by writing the correct letter in the blank.

A. 𝄢

B. ♭

C. 𝄐 (fermata over whole note)

D. *f*

E. 4/4

F. ♮

G. (treble clef on staff)

H. *p*

I. (repeat sign)

J. 8ᵛᵃ

K. (accent note)

L. *rit.*

M. ♯

_____ Time Signature

_____ Piano (soft)

_____ Repeat sign

_____ Bass Clef

_____ Octave sign

_____ Key Signature

_____ Accent sign

_____ Natural sign

_____ Fermata (Bird's Eye)

_____ Flat sign

_____ Ritard (slow down)

_____ Sharp sign

_____ Forte (loud)

SHOUTS and Whispers

Write the correct letter next to each term on the right.

A. ▭───────

_____Mezzo Piano (Medium soft)

B. *dim.*

_____Piano (soft)

C. **pp**

_____Decrescendo

D. 𝅘𝅥

_____Mezzo Forte (Medium Loud)

E. **f**

_____Fortissimo (Very Loud)

F. ───────▭

_____Pianissimo (Very soft)

G. **mf**

_____Accent

H. **p**

_____Staccato Accent

I. **ff**

_____Crescendo

J. **mp**

_____Diminuendo

K. 𝅘𝅥

_____Forte (Loud)

21

RHYTHM SYMBOLS MATCHING

Match the symbols to their names by writing the correct letter in the blank.

A. ♩

B. ♫

C. ♩.

D. 𝄽

E. ▬

F. ♪

G. 𝅝

H. ▬

I. Quarter Note

J. Half Note

K. Whole Note

L. Eighth Note

M. Dotted Half Note

_____ Quarter Note

_____ Half Note

_____ Whole Rest

_____ Quarter Rest

_____ Whole Note

_____ Eighth Notes

_____ Dotted Half Note

_____ Half Rest

_____ Two Beats Each

_____ Three Beats Each

_____ Four Beats Each

_____ Two make a beat

_____ One Beat Each

22

SLICE IT UP IN 4/4!

The pizza represents a MEASURE of music in 4/4 time.
Draw a whole note, half notes, quarter notes and eighth notes
on the correct slices of pizza.

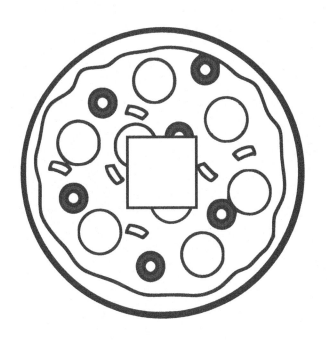
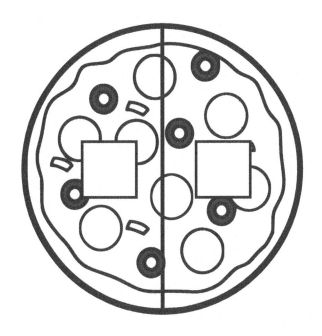

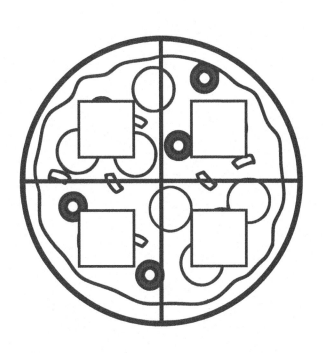

5 FINGER PATTERNS

Fill in the missing letters to complete the spelling of each 5-finger pattern, then HIGHLIGHT the TRIAD NOTES.

C			F	
		F#		A
E	F#			
	G		B♭	
G		B		
A		C#		

24

Fill in the missing letters to complete the spelling of each 5-finger pattern, then HIGHLIGHT the TRIAD NOTES.

			F	
		F#		
E				

			B♭	
		B		
		C#		

Fill in the missing letters to complete the spelling of each
5-finger pattern, then HIGHLIGHT the TRIAD NOTES.

ADD IT UP RHYTHMS

Add together the values of each note in the boxes to the right.
Then add all of the boxes together to see if they equal the total at the bottom.

2
+
4
+
6
+
8

♩ + ♩ + ♫ + 𝄽 = ☐

𝅝 + 𝅝 + ♩ + ♫ = ☐

♩ + ♫ + ♩ + 𝄬 = ☐

♫ + ♫ + ♩ + 𝄬 = ☐

♩ + ♩ + ♫ + 𝄽 = ☐

𝅝 + ♫ + 𝄬 + ♩ = ☐

♩ + ♩ + ♩. + ♫ = ☐

50

SLICE IT UP IN 3/4!

The pizza represents a MEASURE of music in 3/4 time.
Draw a dotted half note, quarter notes and eighth notes
on the correct slices of pizza.

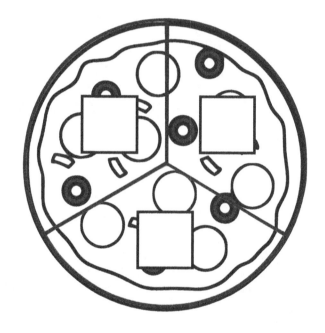

ALPHA-NUMERICS

In music, letters and numbers are used together. Color in the letters and numbers below, using the same color for each letter and it's number.

A B C D E F G

1 2 3 4 5 6 7

29

INTERVALS

An interval is the **distance** between any two pitches.

A HARMONIC interval is two pitches played at the same time.
A MELODIC interval is two pitches played one after the other.

When 2 pitches are BOTH on lines or spaces, they are an **odd-numbered interval** (a 3rd, 5th or 7th).
When 2 pitches are NOT both on lines or spaces (one on a line, and one on a space)
they are an **even-numbered interval**, (a 2nd, 4th, 6th or Octave).
Write a number below each example to show the interval distance between the notes.

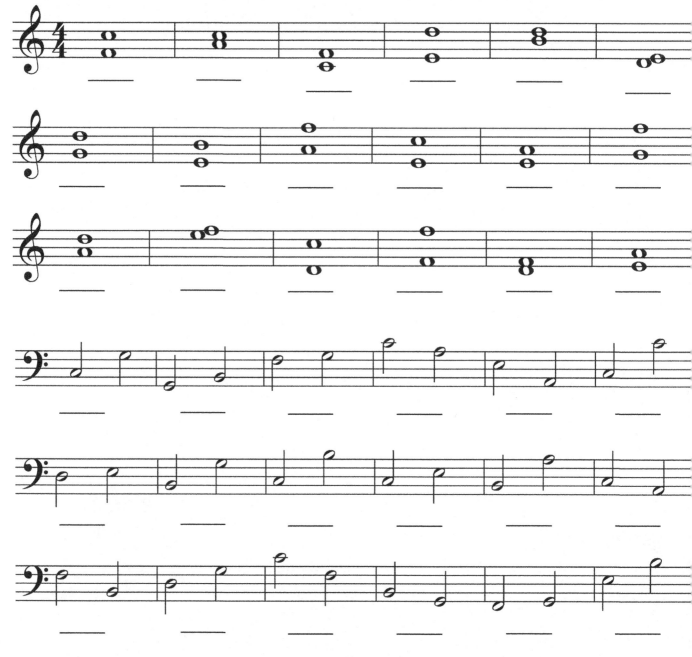

30

HARMONIC INTERVALS

Write a number under each interval to show the distance between the notes.

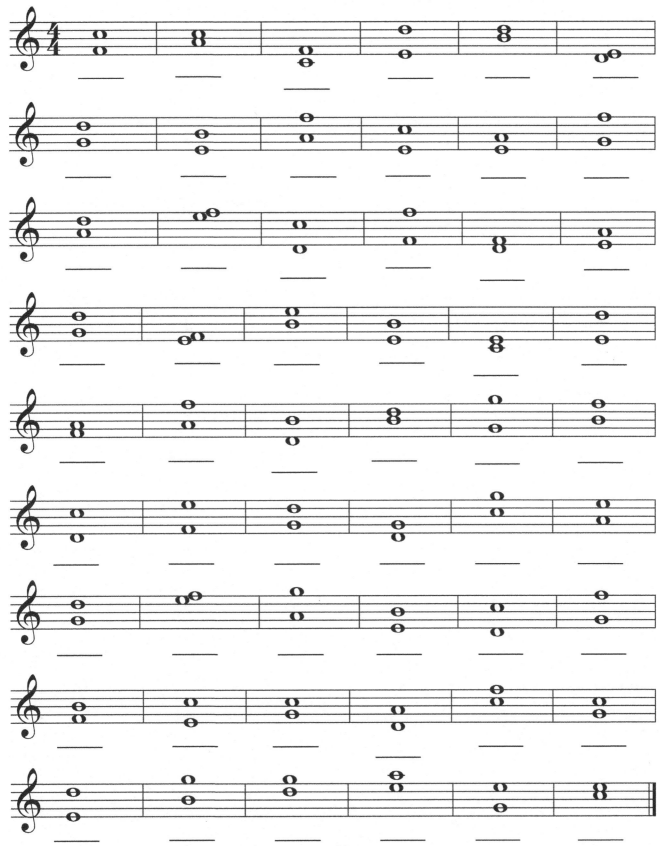

MELODIC INTERVALS

Write a number under each interval to show the distance between the notes.

MUSICAL INSTRUMENT WORDFIND

Words can be spelled forwards, backwards, vertically, horizontally and diagonally.

Saxophone
Synthesizer
Clarinet
Trombone
Percussion
Guitar
Ukulele
Piccolos
Flute
Bassoon

Harp

Violin

Tubas
Drum
Oboe
Kazoo
Piano
Brass
Alto
Bass
Woodwinds
Xylophone

S	A	X	O	P	H	O	N	E	M	Y	E	W
A	Y	Z	B	A	S	S	O	O	N	C	L	O
E	K	N	C	H	J	L	U	B	V	X	E	O
N	G	R	T	R	O	M	B	O	N	E	L	D
O	U	A	U	H	O	R	T	O	W	L	U	W
H	I	O	H	T	E	V	I	Z	F	A	K	I
P	T	F	L	T	I	S	H	A	R	P	U	N
O	A	A	U	O	S	S	I	K	M	U	R	D
L	R	L	L	U	S	A	H	Z	J	H	U	S
Y	F	I	C	L	A	R	I	N	E	T	M	S
X	N	R	R	E	K	B	R	H	P	R	Q	A
I	E	U	B	O	N	A	I	P	T	W	E	B
P	I	C	C	O	L	O	S	A	B	U	T	S

CHROMATIC COASTER

The chromatic scale is a series of 12 tones in consecutive half-steps.

When naming the notes in the chromatic scale, use **sharps** as you ascend and **flats** as you descend.

Remember the half steps between the letters B and C and also the letters E and F have no sharp or flat in between them; these are called *natural half steps*.

Fill in the boxes below with the spelling of the Chromatic scale.
Practice reciting the Chromatic scale out loud as you play the notes on your instrument.

Ascending

| C | | | | | | | | | | | |

Descending

| C | | | | | | | | | | | |

Ascending

| C | | | | | | | | | | | |

Descending

| C | | | | | | | | | | | |

Rainbow Piano

Color all the F's DARK RED.

Color all the G's ORANGE.

Color all the A's GREEN.

Color all the B's DARK BLUE.

Color all the C's BRIGHT RED.

Color all the D's YELLOW.

Color all the E's LIGHT BLUE.

Lines and Spaces
of the Treble Clef

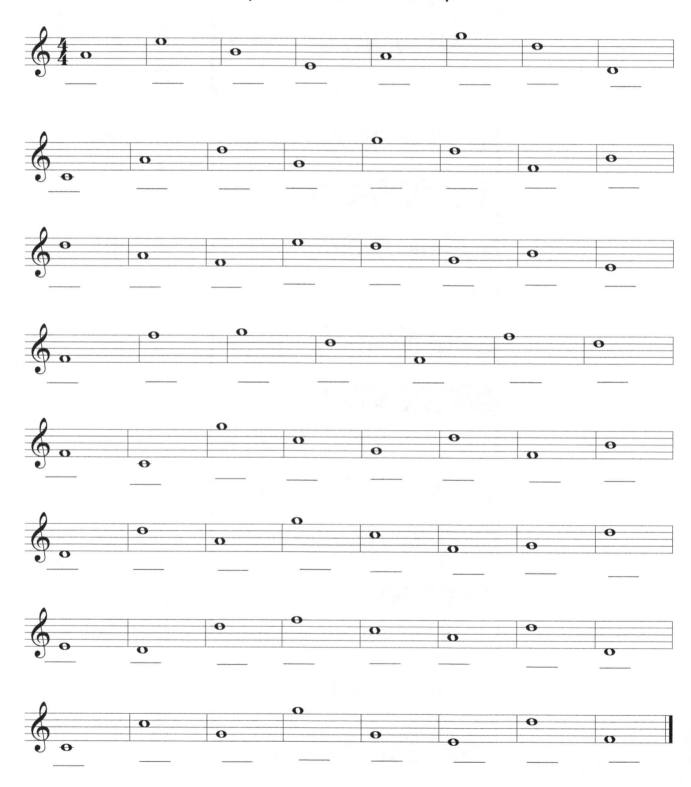

Lines:
EGBDF

Lines and Spaces
of the Treble Clef

Spaces:
FACE

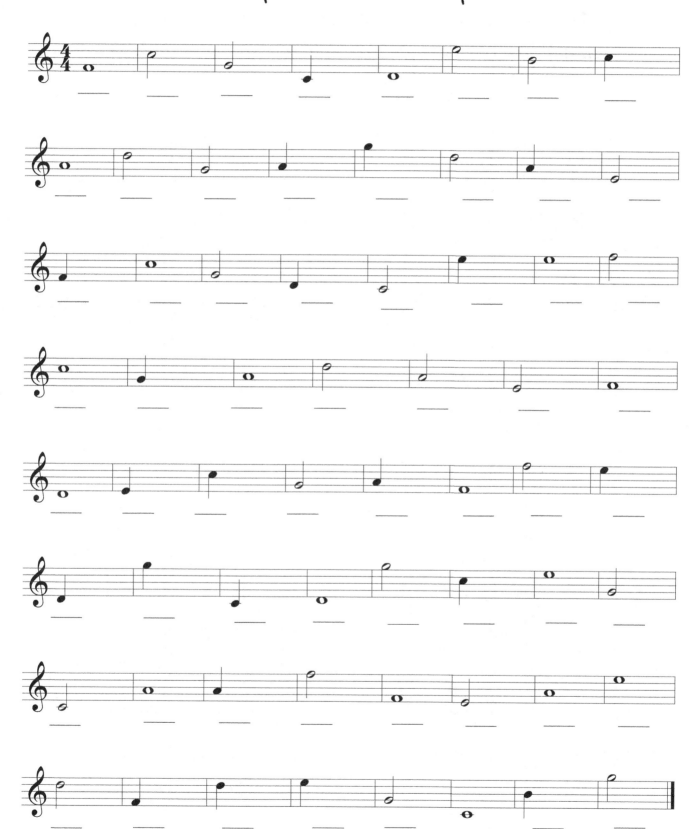

37

SLICE IT UP IN 6/8!

The pizza represents a MEASURE of music in 6/8 time.
Draw a dotted half note, dotted quarter notes, quarter notes and
eighth notes on the correct slices of pizza.

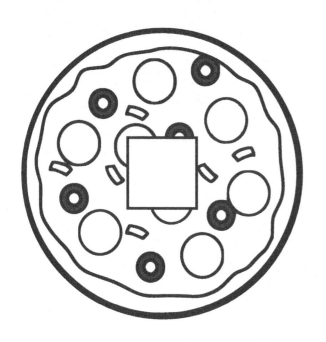
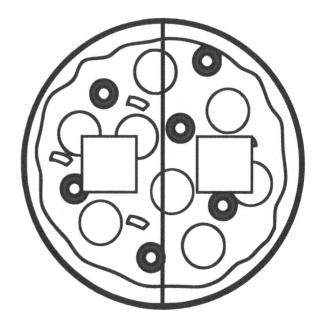

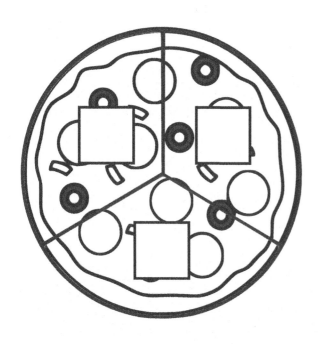

ALPHABET WORD SCRAMBLE

How many words can you spell using **ONLY** the letters of the musical alphabet?
You can use each letter more than once in a word.

A B C D E F G

1. _____

2. _____

3. _____

4. _____

5. _____

6. _____

7. _____

8. _____

9. _____

10. _____

11. _____

12. _____

13. _____

14. _____

15. _____

16. _____

17. _____

18. _____

19. _____

20. _____

21. _____

22. _____

23. _____

24. _____

25. _____

26. _____

27. _____

28. _____

29. _____

30. _____

31. _____

32. _____

33. _____

34. _____

35. _____

36. _____

37. _____

38. _____

39. _____

40. _____

41. _____

42. _____

43. _____

44. _____

45. _____

46. _____

47. _____

48. _____

49. _____

50. _____

51. _____

Lines:
GBDFA

Lines and Spaces
of the Bass Clef

Spaces:
ACEG

40

Lines:
GBDFA

Lines and Spaces
of the Bass Clef

Spaces:
ACEG

41

MUSICAL PATTERN HANGMAN

Fill in the words to describe each pattern. The first letter of each word is given.

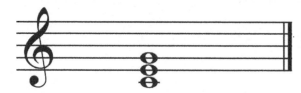

___ M_____ S_____ T_____

W_____ N_____

___ M_____ B_____ T_____

Q_____ N_____

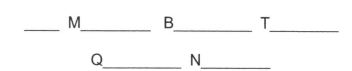

___ M_____ S_____ T_____

W_____ N_____

___ M_____ B_____ T_____

Q_____ N_____

___ M_____ S_____ T_____

H_____ N_____

U_____ ___ M_____

___ F_____ P_____

U_____ ___ M_____

___ F_____ P_____

MUSIC GENRES WORDFIND

HipHop
House
Southern Rock
Funk
Rockabilly
Rhythm and Blues
Opera
Folk
Rock
Emo

Salsa
Ragtime
Classical
DooWop
Jazz
Pop
Ska
Reggae
Punk
Rap

Bluegrass
New Age
Broadway
Surf
BeBop
Soul
Disco
Gospel
Country
Heavy Metal

H	I	P	H	O	P	E	R	A	R	O	W	R
E	Y	G	O	S	P	E	L	A	C	B	K	H
A	A	H	U	F	R	M	P	S	R	C	F	Y
V	W	M	S	P	E	O	I	X	O	N	S	T
Y	D	P	E	O	G	D	V	R	C	K	S	H
M	A	O	U	B	G	S	N	J	K	C	A	M
E	O	W	S	E	A	R	Z	P	A	L	R	A
T	R	O	P	B	E	A	C	Y	B	A	G	N
A	B	O	E	H	Y	G	R	K	I	S	E	D
L	P	D	T	D	R	T	O	N	L	S	U	B
A	F	U	N	K	N	I	C	U	L	I	L	L
K	O	F	R	U	S	M	K	P	Y	C	B	U
S	L	S	O	U	L	E	N	E	W	A	G	E
Q	K	C	J	A	Z	Z	D	A	S	L	A	S

TRIAD INVERSIONS

An inversion is the SAME three notes of a triad, arranged into a new shape.
There are three different shapes of inversions.

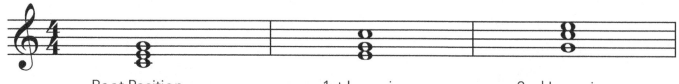

Root Position	1st Inversion	2nd Inversion
"The Snowman"	"Skinny Bottom"	"Fat Bottom"
Root on the BOTTOM	Root on the TOP	Root in the MIDDLE

Write an "R" for root position, "1" for 1st inversion, and "2" for 2nd inversion chords.
Then highlight the ROOT note in each inversion.

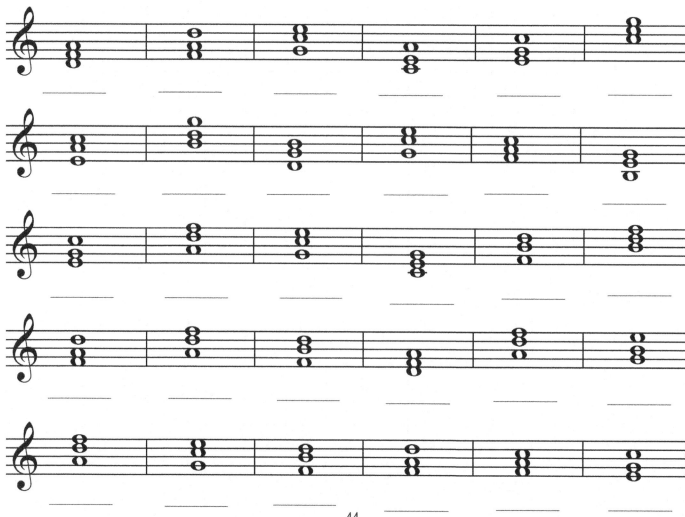

44

MORE TRIAD INVERSIONS

Write an R for ROOT, (1) for 1st inversion and (2) for second inversion shapes.
Then highlight the root note of each triad.

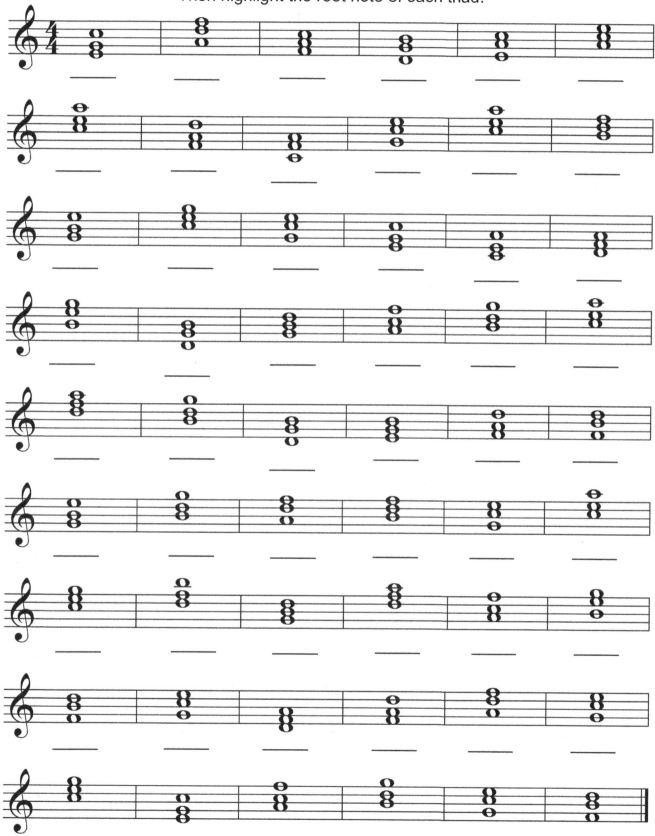

Music Magic Numbers

Fill the correct numbers in the box on the right for each question. Then add the numbers to see if they equal the correct total at the bottom.

1. How many letters are in the music alphabet? ☐

2. How many notes are in a major scale? ☐

3. How many notes are in a minor scale? ☐

4. How many notes are in a major triad? ☐

5. How many notes are in a minor triad? ☐

6. How many notes (1/2 steps) are in the chromatic scale? + ☐

TOTAL: 39

MUSIC TERMS CROSSWORD

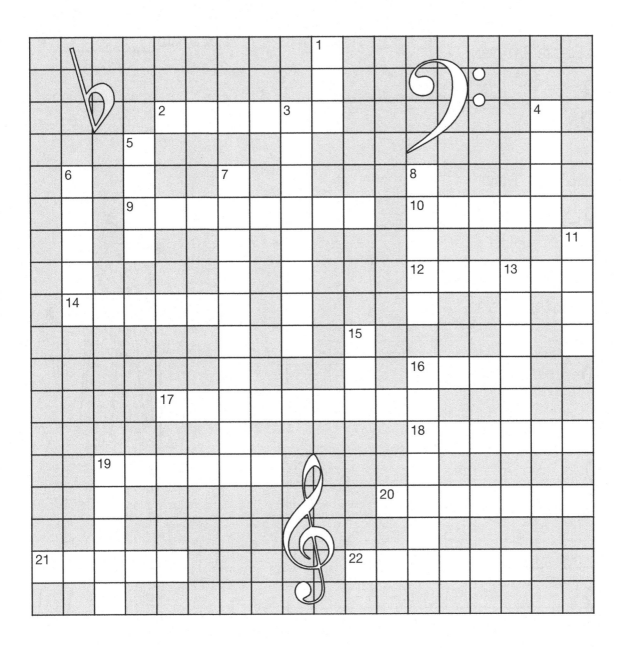

ACROSS

2. The part you sing.
9. Short, detached notes.
10. Bass and treble are types of these.
12. Smooth, connected notes.
14. To slow down gradually.
16. The chord that leads to the "One" chord.
17. They go "beep beep" or "tick tock".
18. Another word for the beat.
19. The clef for high notes.
20. Two chords that build tension, then resolve.
21. Sharps and _____.
22. Lines and _____.

DOWN

1. The seven notes of a scale make up a _____.
3. How loudly and softly the notes are played.
4. Another word for measures.
5. The clef for low notes.
6. The happy sounding chord or key.
7. A sharp or flat that is not from the key.
8. Seven steps in a row.
11. The symbol that points to the ending.
13. Playing a note louder than the notes around it.
15. In 4/4 time, a half note gets _____ beats.
16. A symbol for holding a note or rest.
19. A three-note chord.

IT'S A DRAW! MUSICAL PATTERNS

KEY OF:_____

FIVE FINGER PATTERN:

SOLID MAJOR TRIAD:

BROKEN MAJOR TRIAD:

MAJOR TRIAD INVERSIONS:

PRIMARY CHORDS: I - IV - V

MAJOR SCALE:

ALBERTI BASS:

48

IT'S A DRAW! MUSICAL PATTERNS

KEY OF:_____

FIVE FINGER PATTERN:

SOLID MAJOR TRIAD:

BROKEN MAJOR TRIAD:

MAJOR TRIAD INVERSIONS:

PRIMARY CHORDS: I -   IV   -   V

MAJOR SCALE:

ALBERTI BASS:

49

IT'S A DRAW! MUSICAL PATTERNS

KEY OF: _____

FIVE FINGER PATTERN:

SOLID MAJOR TRIAD:

BROKEN MAJOR TRIAD:

MAJOR TRIAD INVERSIONS:

PRIMARY CHORDS: I -   IV   -   V

MAJOR SCALE:

ALBERTI BASS:

50

It's a Draw! Musical Patterns

Key of: _____

Five Finger Pattern:

Solid Major Triad:

Broken Major Triad:

Major Triad Inversions:

Primary Chords: I - IV - V

Major Scale:

Alberti Bass:

51

It's a Draw! Musical Patterns

KEY OF: _____

FIVE FINGER PATTERN:

SOLID MAJOR TRIAD:

BROKEN MAJOR TRIAD:

MAJOR TRIAD INVERSIONS:

PRIMARY CHORDS: I -   IV   -   V

MAJOR SCALE:

ALBERTI BASS:

52

MUSICAL INSTRUMENT CROSSWORD

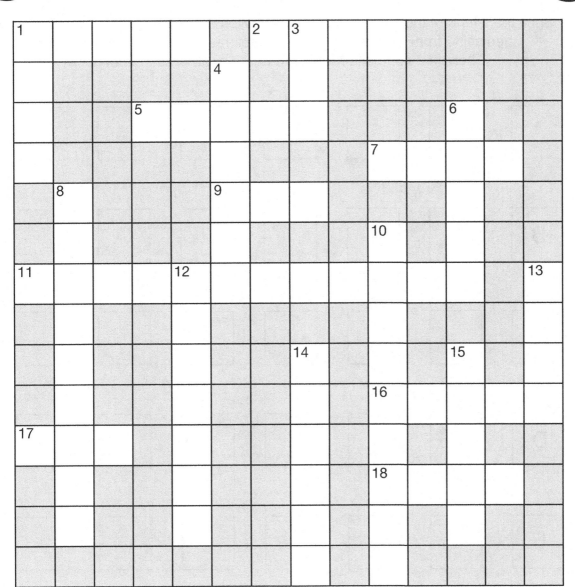

ACROSS

1. Stringed instrument with a drum for a body.
2. Large brass instrument worn across the body.
5. A woodwind usually made of silver.
7. French _____.
9. A small drum; also a boy's name.
11. The lowest string instrument in a rock band.
12. A wooden keyboard played with mallets.
16. Has 88 notes, more than any instrument.
17. Used to strike the strings of a violin.
18. Small double reed instrument made of wood.

DOWN

1. Cow, hand, and church are kinds of these.
3. A small Hawaiian string instrument.
4. 6-stringed instrument with a hollow body.
6. The very first musical instruments.
8. A metal keyboard played with mallets.
10. A reed instrument made of brass.
12. A brass instrument with three valves.
13. The smaller, higher sounding saxophone.
14. Used to strike percussion instruments.
15. An instrument you "hum" into.

ALPHABET SOUP

Spell the letters of the musical alphabet in **EVERY OTHER LETTER ORDER**, beginning from each letter. Time yourself reading the entire page.
Then time yourself reading the entire page from memory!

A						

B						

C						

D						

E						

F						

G						

TRIAD SPELLING MASTER

REMEMBER ALPHABET SOUP: A C E G B D F

KEY	MAJOR	MINOR
C		
G		
D		
A		
E		
B		
F$^\#$		
C$^\#$		
C$^\flat$		
G$^\flat$		
D$^\flat$		
A$^\flat$		
E$^\flat$		
B$^\flat$		
F		

MAJOR TRIAD WORD FIND

Triads can be spelled vertically, horizontally, diagonally, forwards and backwards.

TIME:_____

C	A	C	G	E	F♯	F	E♭	A	B♭
A	E	A	B♭	A♯	A	D♯	G	G	G
F♯	C	G	C♯	E♭	B	A	E♭	E	A
G♭	E	A	G	D	D♭	F	A♭	B	F
E♭	B♭	E	G♯	B	E♭	C	F	D♯	C♯
C♭	C♯	D♭	F	D♭	B	D	A	E♭	A
D♭	A	C♯	E	G	B♭	F♯	C	B♭	F♯
G	F♯	G	C♭	F♯	B	A♭	D♭	G♯	D♯
F♯	D	B	G	B♭	G♯	E♯	C♯	A♭	B
A	F	G♭	D♯	G	D♭	F	E♭	D	A♯

56

MINOR TRIAD WORD FIND

Triads can be spelled vertically, horizontally, diagonally, forwards and backwards.

TIME:_____

E♭	G♭	B♭	A	C	A♯	B	D	F♯	G
A	D	G	D	C♭	D	B	A	C	F
C	B	E♭	B	E♭♭	B	F	G	E	G♭
F♯	A	C	F	G♭	D	A	F	B♭♭	D
A♭	G	E♯	B♭	A	C♯	G	D♭	C	F
C♭	B	G	D♭	E	G	B♭	D	B	G
E♭	A	B	F	D	B	F	A♭	C	D♯
C	F	C	A	C	A	F♭	C	G	F
D♯	B	D	E	F	D♭	G	B	E♯	C
D	G♯	E	C♯	A	F♯	A	E	G	B

STEPS TO SPELL TRIADS

Use the last letter of each triad to spell the next triad on the puzzle until you have spelled all 15 major triads in music. The first one is given.

Find the Root

Circle which of the three letters is the **ROOT** note of each of these major triads.

G E C   C A F

B G D   G# E B

C# E A   A F# D

C F A   B♭ D F   B♭ D♭ G♭

C♭ G♭ E♭   E♭ G♭ C♭   C# E# G#

A C# E   B F# D#   E♭ C A♭

G D B   G E♭ B♭   A♭ F D♭

MIXED-UP TRIADS

All types of triads - major, minor, diminished and augmented, have the same set of three letters in them, regardless of any sharps or flats.

Circle all of the **G type** triads:

B D G	D F A	G E B	D F B
C E G	C A E	D G B	A C E
C F A	G E C	C G E	B G D
E G B	G B D	C E A	B E G
D B G	B D F	F D A	A F D
G E C	A E C	G D B	B G E

Circle all of the **E type** triads:

C E G	C E A	E G B	D F B
G E B	B F D	G C E	E C G
F A C	B E G	F C A	E A C
F A D	C G E	D B G	C E G
G D B	F D A	B D F	B G E
A E C	F B D	D G B	A C E

What's That Word?

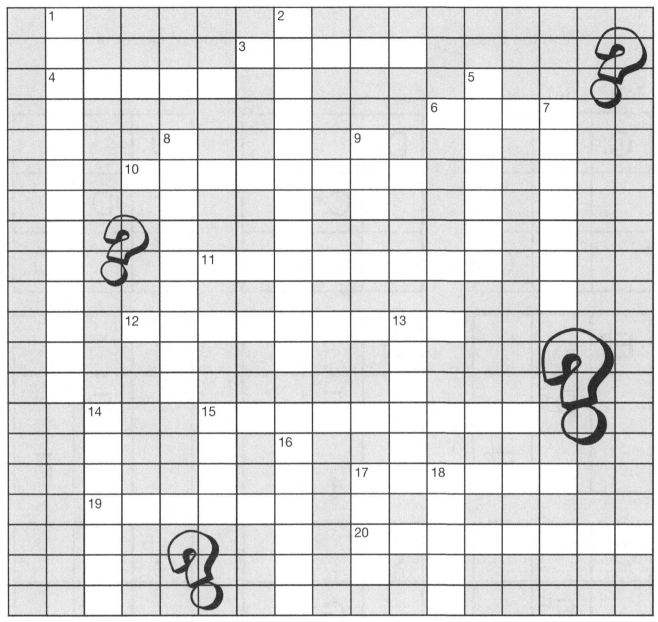

ACROSS

3. Grouping the beat.
4. The sad sounding triad or key.
6. The lowest voice in a 4-note chord.
10. A broken chord.
11. The distance between two pitches.
12. A chord turned upside down.
15. Scale with 12 consecutive half steps.
17. Symbol that says "play it again".
19. Piece with 3 sections for solo instrument.
20. A repeating figure, usually in the bass.

DOWN

1. Shows how many beats in a measure.
2. Shows the sharps or flats for each key.
5. Cancels an accidental.
7. The highest voice in a 4-note chord.
8. Gradually getting louder.
9. Turns 2 short notes into one long note.
13. Two notes 8 steps apart.
14. Another name for bars in music.
15. Symbol that means "the ending".
16. _____ and flats.
17. The naming note of a chord.
18. Another name for "note".

MAJOR TRIAD SUDOKU

Fill in the missing pitch to complete the spelling of each triad.

Root   3rd   5th

C		
	C	
		C

D♭		
	C♯	
		D♭

D		
	D	
		D

E♭		
	D♯	
		E♭

E		
	E	
		E

F		
	F	
		F

G♭		
	F♯	
		F♯

G		
	G	
		G

A♭		
	G♯	
		A♭

A		
	A	
		A

B♭		
	B♭	
		B♭

B		
	B	
		B

MINOR TRIAD SUDOKU

Fill in the missing pitch to complete the spelling of each triad.

Root   3rd   5th

Root	3rd	5th
C		
	C	
		C

Root	3rd	5th
D♭		
	D♭	
		D♭

Root	3rd	5th
D		
	D	
		D

Root	3rd	5th
E♭		
	E♭	
		E♭

Root	3rd	5th
E		
	E	
		E

Root	3rd	5th
F		
	F	
		F

Root	3rd	5th
G♭		
	G♭	
		F♯

Root	3rd	5th
G		
	G	
		G

Root	3rd	5th
A♭		
	A♭	
		A♭

Root	3rd	5th
A		
	A	
		A

Root	3rd	5th
B♭		
	B♭	
		B♭

Root	3rd	5th
B		
	C♭	
		B

Music Magic Numbers

Fill the correct numbers in the box on the right for each question. Then add the numbers to see if they equal the correct total at the bottom.

1. How many letters are in the music alphabet? ☐

2. How many notes are in a key? ☐

3. How many major triads are in a key? ☐

4. How many minor triads are in a key? ☐

5. How many diminished triads are in a key? ☐

6. How many major keys are there in music? ☐

7. How many minor keys are there in music? ☐

8. How many notes are in the chromatic scale? + ☐

TOTAL: 63

64

The Order of Sharps and Flats

Write the correct letters in the boxes on the right to show
the sharps or flats that are in that key. The first one is given.

MINOR   MAJOR

MINOR	MAJOR
d	F
g	B♭
c	E♭
f	A♭
b♭	D♭
e♭	G♭
a♭	C♭
a	C
e	G
b	D
f#	A
c#	E
g#	B
d#	F#
a#	C#

B♭

65

KEY SIGNATURE IDENTIFICATION

Identify each key signature. Write both the major and minor key for each.

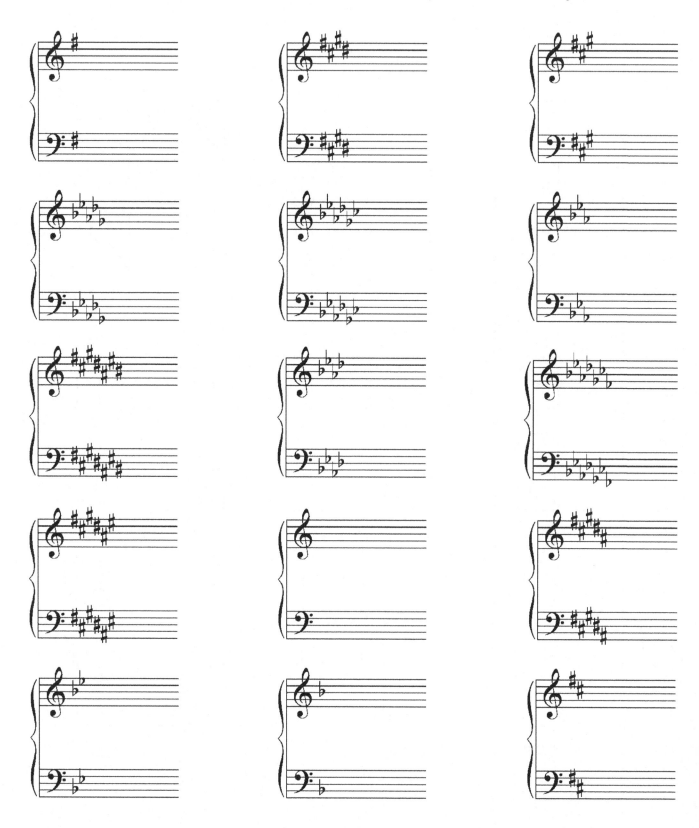

DRAWING KEY SIGNATURES

Draw the sharps or flats for each key signature in the correct order for each example.

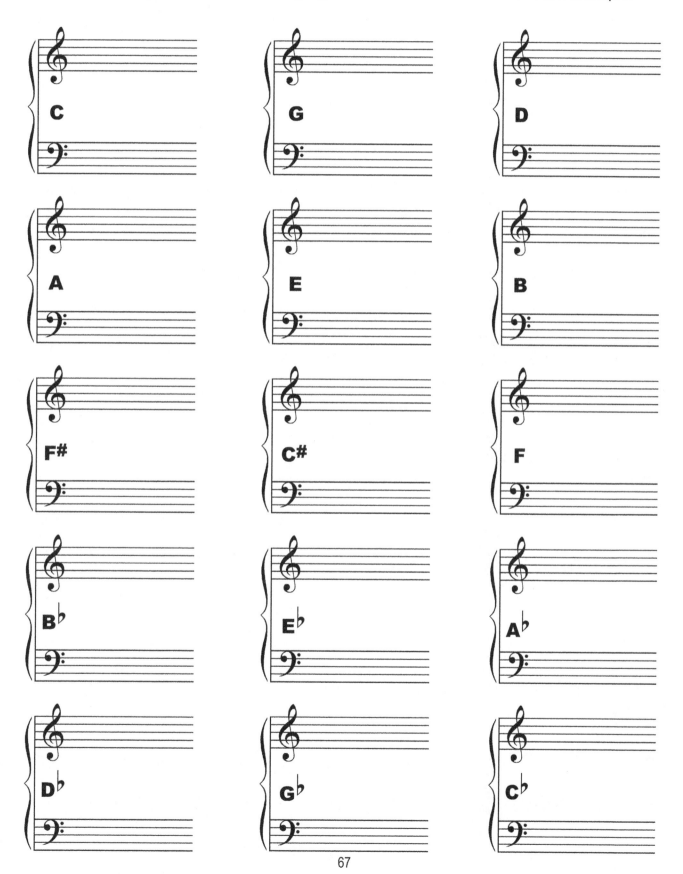

Writing Sharp Key Scales

Write the notes of each scale in whole notes, using accidentals.

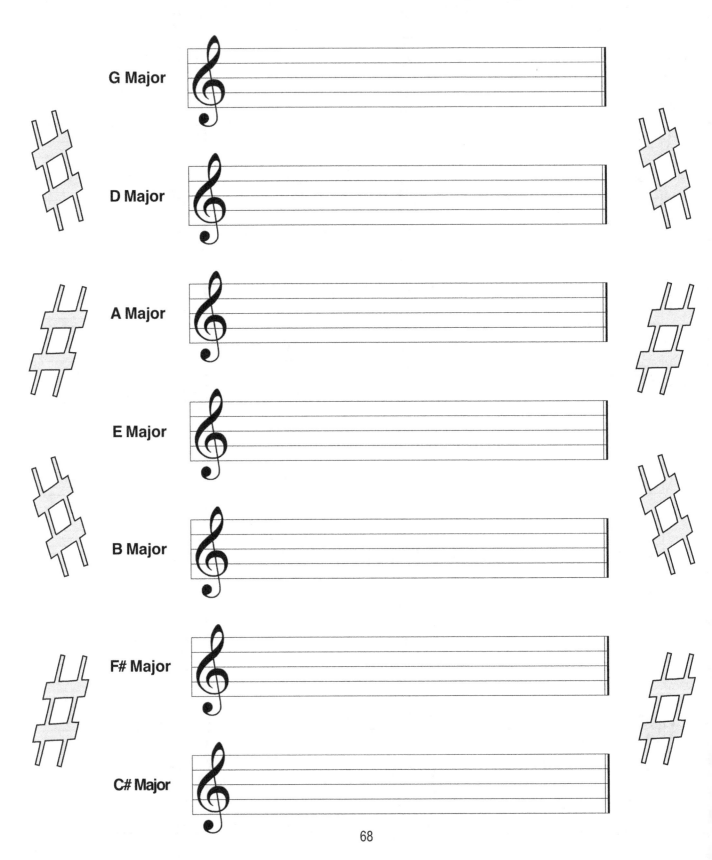

G Major

D Major

A Major

E Major

B Major

F# Major

C# Major

Writing Flat Key Scales

Write the notes of each scale in whole notes, using accidentals.

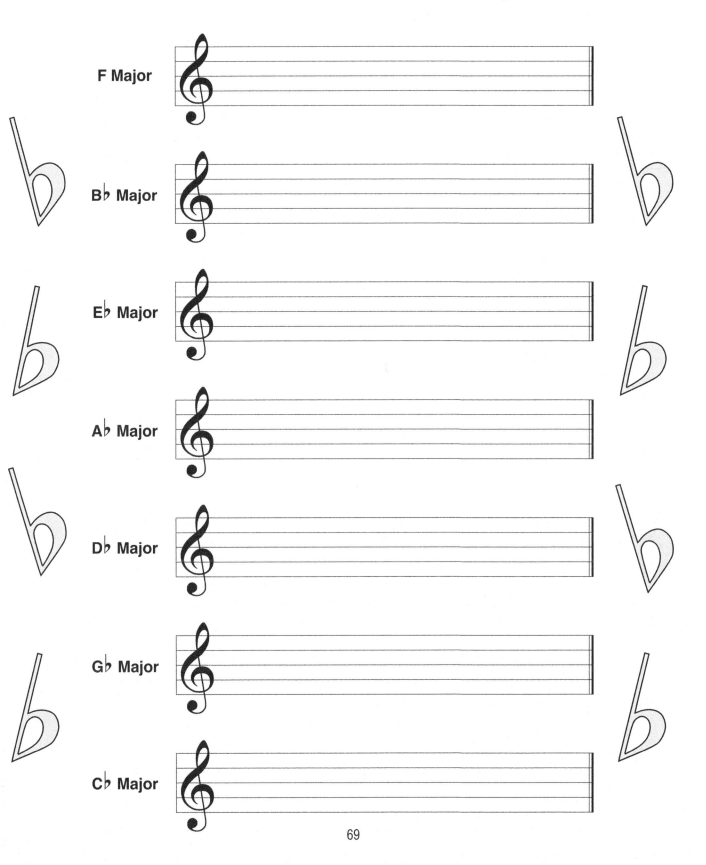

Fill in the boxes with the correct letters or numbers to learn this key INSIDE OUT!

1. SPELL IT OUT with accidentals:

KEY : _____

4. SAY IT AND PLAY IT ON YOUR INSTRUMENT.

2. PUT A CHECK IN THE BOX for each time you Spell it OUT LOUD:

1	2	3	4	5	6	7	8	9	10

11	12	13	14	15	16	17	18	19	20

3. NAME each DEGREE of the scale by matching the number with the letter names:

3	7	1	5	2	6	4

2	5	3	7	4	6	1

7	4	2	6	1	5	3

4	6	2	5	1	3	7

1	3	2	6	4	7	5

1	6	2	5	3	7	4

5	2	6	4	7	3	1

5	1	4	7	3	6	2

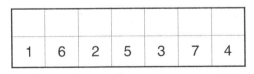

70

Fill in the boxes with the correct letters or numbers to learn this key INSIDE OUT!

1. SPELL IT OUT with accidentals:

4. SAY IT
AND
PLAY IT
ON YOUR
INSTRUMENT.

2. PUT A CHECK IN THE BOX for each time you Spell it OUT LOUD:

1	2	3	4	5	6	7	8	9	10

11	12	13	14	15	16	17	18	19	20

3. NAME each DEGREE of the scale by matching the number with the letter names:

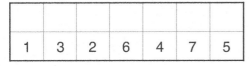

3	7	1	5	2	6	4

2	5	3	7	4	6	1

7	4	2	6	1	5	3

4	6	2	5	1	3	7

1	3	2	6	4	7	5

1	6	2	5	3	7	4

5	2	6	4	7	3	1

5	1	4	7	3	6	2

71

Fill in the boxes with the correct letters or numbers to learn this key INSIDE OUT!

1. SPELL IT OUT with accidentals:

KEY : _____

4. SAY IT AND PLAY IT ON YOUR INSTRUMENT.

2. PUT A CHECK IN THE BOX for each time you Spell it OUT LOUD:

1	2	3	4	5	6	7	8	9	10

11	12	13	14	15	16	17	18	19	20

3. NAME each DEGREE of the scale by matching the number with the letter names:

3	7	1	5	2	6	4

2	5	3	7	4	6	1

7	4	2	6	1	5	3

4	6	2	5	1	3	7

1	3	2	6	4	7	5

1	6	2	5	3	7	4

5	2	6	4	7	3	1

5	1	4	7	3	6	2

72

A KEY A DAY

Fill in the boxes with the correct letters or numbers to learn this key INSIDE OUT!

1. SPELL IT OUT with accidentals:

KEY : _____

4. SAY IT
AND
PLAY IT
ON YOUR
INSTRUMENT.

2. PUT A CHECK IN THE BOX for each time you Spell it OUT LOUD:

1	2	3	4	5	6	7	8	9	10

11	12	13	14	15	16	17	18	19	20

3. NAME each DEGREE of the scale by matching the number with the letter names:

3	7	1	5	2	6	4

2	5	3	7	4	6	1

7	4	2	6	1	5	3

4	6	2	5	1	3	7

1	3	2	6	4	7	5

1	6	2	5	3	7	4

5	2	6	4	7	3	1

5	1	4	7	3	6	2

#

Fill in the boxes with the correct letters or numbers to learn this key INSIDE OUT!

1. SPELL IT OUT with accidentals:

KEY : _____

4. SAY IT AND PLAY IT ON YOUR INSTRUMENT.

2. PUT A CHECK IN THE BOX for each time you Spell it OUT LOUD:

1	2	3	4	5	6	7	8	9	10

11	12	13	14	15	16	17	18	19	20

3. NAME each DEGREE of the scale by matching the number with the letter names:

3	7	1	5	2	6	4

2	5	3	7	4	6	1

7	4	2	6	1	5	3

4	6	2	5	1	3	7

1	3	2	6	4	7	5

1	6	2	5	3	7	4

5	2	6	4	7	3	1

5	1	4	7	3	6	2

Fill in the boxes with the correct letters or numbers to learn this key INSIDE OUT!

1. SPELL IT OUT with accidentals:

KEY : _____

4. SAY IT
AND
PLAY IT
ON YOUR
INSTRUMENT.

2. PUT A CHECK IN THE BOX for each time you Spell it OUT LOUD:

1	2	3	4	5	6	7	8	9	10

11	12	13	14	15	16	17	18	19	20

3. NAME each DEGREE of the scale by matching the number with the letter names:

3	7	1	5	2	6	4

2	5	3	7	4	6	1

7	4	2	6	1	5	3

4	6	2	5	1	3	7

1	3	2	6	4	7	5

1	6	2	5	3	7	4

5	2	6	4	7	3	1

5	1	4	7	3	6	2

A KEY A DAY

Fill in the boxes with the correct letters or numbers to learn this key INSIDE OUT!

1. SPELL IT OUT with accidentals:

KEY : _____

4. SAY IT
AND
PLAY IT
ON YOUR
INSTRUMENT.

2. PUT A CHECK IN THE BOX for each time you Spell it OUT LOUD:

1	2	3	4	5	6	7	8	9	10

11	12	13	14	15	16	17	18	19	20

3. NAME each DEGREE of the scale by matching the number with the letter names:

3	7	1	5	2	6	4

2	5	3	7	4	6	1

7	4	2	6	1	5	3

4	6	2	5	1	3	7

1	3	2	6	4	7	5

1	6	2	5	3	7	4

5	2	6	4	7	3	1

5	1	4	7	3	6	2

Fill in the boxes with the correct letters or numbers to learn this key INSIDE OUT!

1. SPELL IT OUT with accidentals:

KEY : _____

4. SAY IT
AND
PLAY IT
ON YOUR
INSTRUMENT.

2. PUT A CHECK IN THE BOX for each time you Spell it OUT LOUD:

1	2	3	4	5	6	7	8	9	10

11	12	13	14	15	16	17	18	19	20

3. NAME each DEGREE of the scale by matching the number with the letter names:

3	7	1	5	2	6	4

2	5	3	7	4	6	1

7	4	2	6	1	5	3

4	6	2	5	1	3	7

1	3	2	6	4	7	5

1	6	2	5	3	7	4

5	2	6	4	7	3	1

5	1	4	7	3	6	2

#

Fill in the boxes with the correct letters or numbers to learn this key INSIDE OUT!

1. SPELL IT OUT with accidentals:

KEY : _____

4. SAY IT AND PLAY IT ON YOUR INSTRUMENT.

2. PUT A CHECK IN THE BOX for each time you Spell it OUT LOUD:

1	2	3	4	5	6	7	8	9	10

11	12	13	14	15	16	17	18	19	20

3. NAME each DEGREE of the scale by matching the number with the letter names:

3	7	1	5	2	6	4

2	5	3	7	4	6	1

7	4	2	6	1	5	3

4	6	2	5	1	3	7

1	3	2	6	4	7	5

1	6	2	5	3	7	4

5	2	6	4	7	3	1

5	1	4	7	3	6	2

Fill in the boxes with the correct letters or numbers to learn this key INSIDE OUT!

1. SPELL IT OUT with accidentals:

KEY : _____

4. SAY IT AND PLAY IT ON YOUR INSTRUMENT.

2. PUT A CHECK IN THE BOX for each time you Spell it OUT LOUD:

1	2	3	4	5	6	7	8	9	10

11	12	13	14	15	16	17	18	19	20

3. NAME each DEGREE of the scale by matching the number with the letter names:

3	7	1	5	2	6	4

2	5	3	7	4	6	1

7	4	2	6	1	5	3

4	6	2	5	1	3	7

1	3	2	6	4	7	5

1	6	2	5	3	7	4

5	2	6	4	7	3	1

5	1	4	7	3	6	2

A KEY A DAY

Fill in the boxes with the correct letters or numbers to learn this key INSIDE OUT!

1. SPELL IT OUT with accidentals:

KEY : _____

4. SAY IT AND PLAY IT ON YOUR INSTRUMENT.

2. PUT A CHECK IN THE BOX for each time you Spell it OUT LOUD:

1	2	3	4	5	6	7	8	9	10

11	12	13	14	15	16	17	18	19	20

3. NAME each DEGREE of the scale by matching the number with the letter names:

3	7	1	5	2	6	4

2	5	3	7	4	6	1

7	4	2	6	1	5	3

4	6	2	5	1	3	7

1	3	2	6	4	7	5

1	6	2	5	3	7	4

5	2	6	4	7	3	1

5	1	4	7	3	6	2

Fill in the boxes with the correct letters or numbers to learn this key INSIDE OUT!

1. SPELL IT OUT with accidentals:

KEY : _____

4. SAY IT AND PLAY IT ON YOUR INSTRUMENT.

2. PUT A CHECK IN THE BOX for each time you Spell it OUT LOUD:

1	2	3	4	5	6	7	8	9	10

11	12	13	14	15	16	17	18	19	20

3. NAME each DEGREE of the scale by matching the number with the letter names:

3	7	1	5	2	6	4

2	5	3	7	4	6	1

7	4	2	6	1	5	3

4	6	2	5	1	3	7

1	3	2	6	4	7	5

1	6	2	5	3	7	4

5	2	6	4	7	3	1

5	1	4	7	3	6	2

Fill in the boxes with the correct letters or numbers to learn this key INSIDE OUT!

1. SPELL IT OUT with accidentals:

KEY : _____

4. SAY IT AND PLAY IT ON YOUR INSTRUMENT.

2. PUT A CHECK IN THE BOX for each time you Spell it OUT LOUD:

1	2	3	4	5	6	7	8	9	10

11	12	13	14	15	16	17	18	19	20

3. NAME each DEGREE of the scale by matching the number with the letter names:

3	7	1	5	2	6	4

2	5	3	7	4	6	1

7	4	2	6	1	5	3

4	6	2	5	1	3	7

1	3	2	6	4	7	5

1	6	2	5	3	7	4

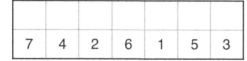
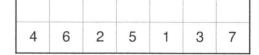

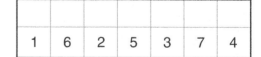

5	2	6	4	7	3	1

5	1	4	7	3	6	2

82

Fill in the boxes with the correct letters or numbers to learn this key INSIDE OUT!

1. SPELL IT OUT with accidentals:

KEY : _____

4. SAY IT AND PLAY IT ON YOUR INSTRUMENT.

2. PUT A CHECK IN THE BOX for each time you Spell it OUT LOUD:

1	2	3	4	5	6	7	8	9	10

11	12	13	14	15	16	17	18	19	20

3. NAME each DEGREE of the scale by matching the number with the letter names:

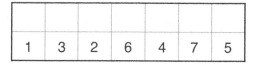

83

A KEY A DAY

Fill in the boxes with the correct letters or numbers to learn this key INSIDE OUT!

1. *SPELL IT OUT with accidentals:*

KEY : _____

> 4. SAY IT
> AND
> PLAY IT
> ON YOUR
> INSTRUMENT.

2. PUT A CHECK IN THE BOX for each time you Spell it OUT LOUD:

1	2	3	4	5	6	7	8	9	10

11	12	13	14	15	16	17	18	19	20

3. NAME each DEGREE of the scale by matching the number with the letter names:

3	7	1	5	2	6	4

2	5	3	7	4	6	1

7	4	2	6	1	5	3

4	6	2	5	1	3	7

1	3	2	6	4	7	5

1	6	2	5	3	7	4

5	2	6	4	7	3	1

5	1	4	7	3	6	2

Composers and their Tools

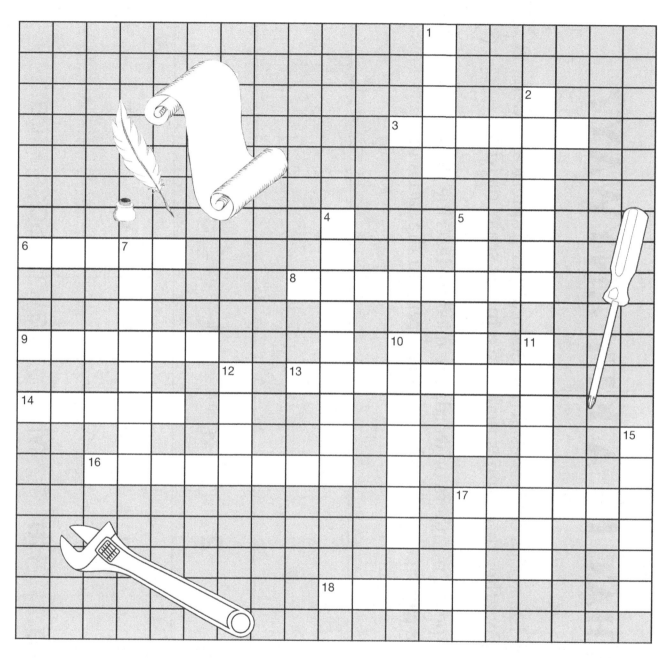

ACROSS

3. Classical era composer who wrote over 500 works.
6. Another name for sheet music.
8. Same melody, different notes.
9. A musical sentence.
13. A little sonata.
14. French contemporary composer.
16. American composer, wrote "Rhapsody in Blue".
17. The part you sing.
18. How fast or slow the piece is played.

DOWN

1. The sad sounding chord or key.
2. A short piece before another piece.
4. Famous composer of the Classical era.
5. How loud or soft the notes are played.
7. A key with the same notes, but different starting note.
10. The chords in a piece of music.
11. A key with different notes, but the same starting note.
12. Famous composer of the Baroque era.
15. The third element of music.
17. The happy sounding chord or key.

WHAT IS A KEY ANYWAY?

A key is a series of 7 tones arranged in alpha-numerical order. Together these tones make up a major scale, or KEY.

Different types of numbers or words are used to describe the notes in a key. The letters can change, but the numbers remain the same in every key.

Letters	C	D	E	F	G	A	B
Degrees	1	2	3	4	5	6	7
Chords	I	ii	iii	IV	V	vi	viiº
Solfegge	Do	Re	Mi	Fa	So	La	Ti

This diagram illustrates the order that the chords of a key tend to "fall" in most songs. Fill in chord symbols (with letters) from the Key of C Major beneath the Roman numerals.

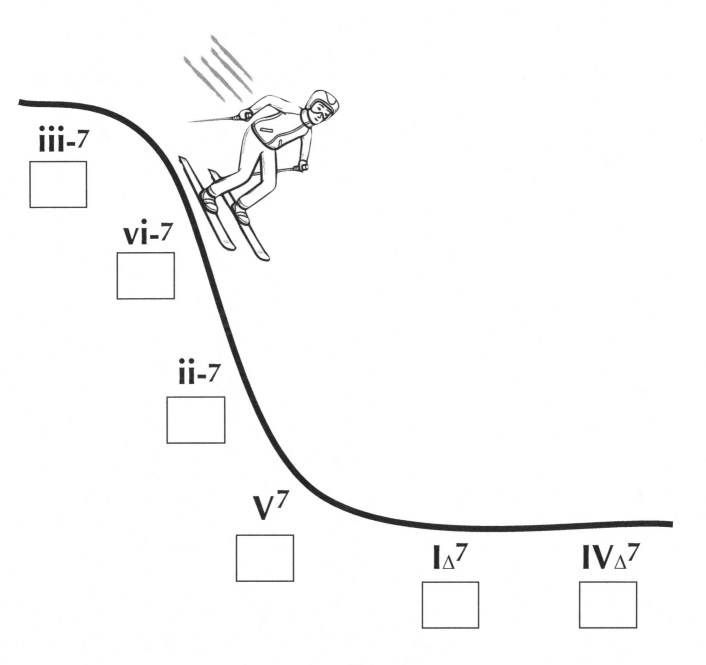

KEY MATRIX

This matrix shows how chords of a key are built using the same 7 notes over and over. The bottom row are the key/scale tones, and the vertical rows are the chord spellings. In music, scales are spelled *alphabetically*, and chords are spelled *every other letter*.

Color all the C's Red. Color all the D's Yellow. Color all the E's Blue. Color all the F's Maroon. Color all the G's Orange. Color all the A's Green. Color all the B's Purple.

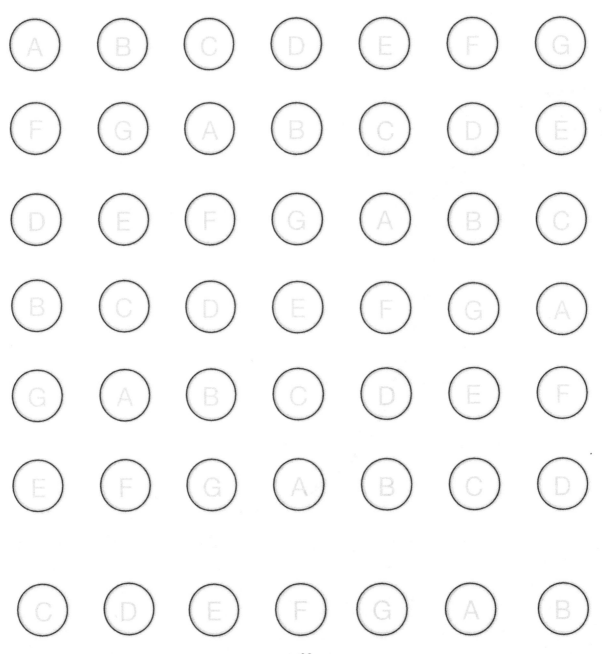

RELATIVE or PARALLEL?

Relative keys have the same 7 notes, but start on a different note.
Parallel keys have different notes, but start on the same note.

1. What is the RELATIVE key of D Major? _____

2. What is the RELATIVE key of G Major? _____

3. What is the RELATIVE key of E Major? _____

4. What is the RELATIVE key of D Minor? _____

5. What is the RELATIVE key of E Minor? _____

6. What is the RELATIVE key of A Minor? _____

7. What is the PARALLEL key of D Major? _____

8. What is the PARALLEL key of B Major? _____

9. What is the PARALLEL key of E Major? _____

10. What is the RELATIVE key of Bb Major? _____

11. What is the RELATIVE key of Eb Major? _____

12. What is the RELATIVE key of Ab Major? _____

13. What is the RELATIVE key of F Minor? _____

14. What is the RELATIVE key of C Minor? _____

15. What is the RELATIVE key of G Minor? _____

16. What is the PARALLEL key of Ab Major? _____

17. What is the PARALLEL key of Eb Major? _____

18. What is the PARALLEL key of C Major? _____

19. What is the RELATIVE key of C Minor? _____

20. What is the PARALLEL key of Eb Major? _____

21. What is the RELATIVE key of Gb Major? _____

22. What is the RELATIVE key of Ab Major? _____

TYPES OF MINOR KEYS

1. What is the Red Flag Note (ACCIDENTAL) in the key of A minor? _____

2. What is the Red Flag Note (ACCIDENTAL) in the key of E minor? _____

3. What is the Red Flag Note (ACCIDENTAL) in the key of G minor? _____

4. What is the Red Flag Note (ACCIDENTAL) in the key of F minor? _____

5. What is the Red Flag Note (ACCIDENTAL) in the key of D minor? _____

6. What is the V chord in the key of A NATURAL minor?

7. What is the V chord in the key of A HARMONIC minor?

8. What is the V chord in the key of E NATURAL minor?

9. What is the V chord in the key of E HARMONIC minor?

10. Write the notes of a C NATURAL minor scale:

11. Write the notes of the G HARMONIC minor scale:

12. Write the notes of the E NATURAL minor scale:

13. Write the notes of the E HARMONIC minor scale:

MUSICAL DNA CHART

Color the Tonic key red, the Dominant blue, the Sub-dominant yellow, the Relative pink and the Parallel key purple.

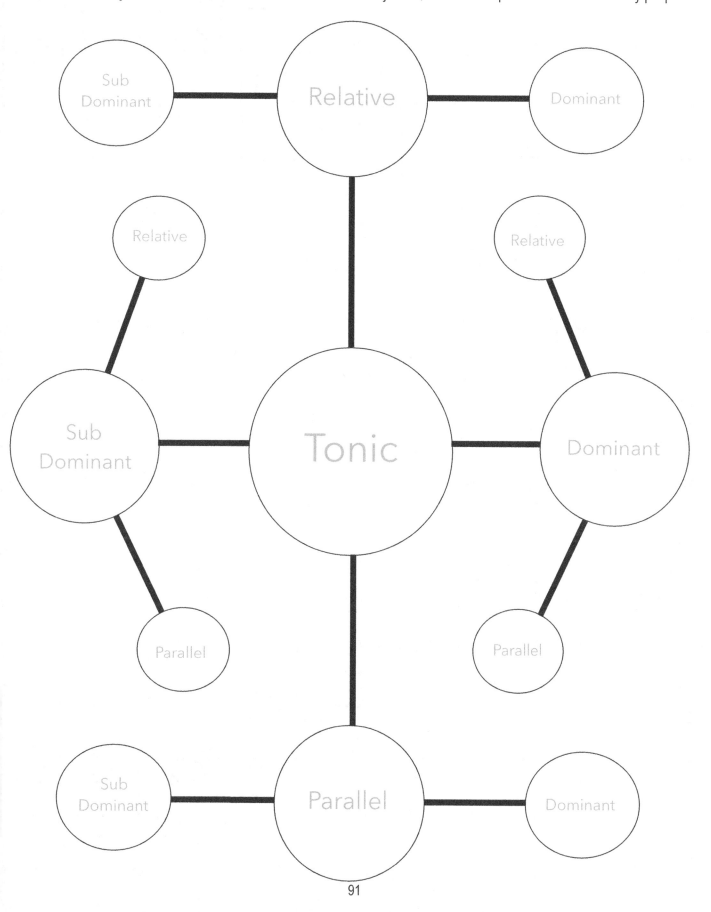

THE KEY SYSTEM IN MUSIC

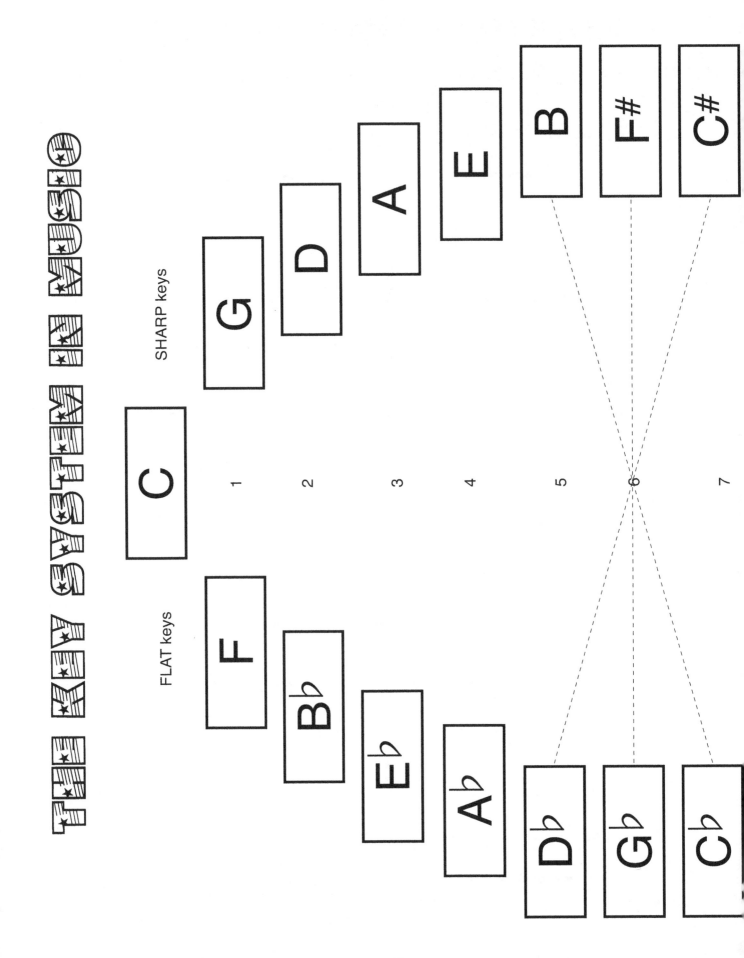

SHARP keys

FLAT keys

C

G

D

A

E

B

F#

C#

F

B♭

E♭

A♭

D♭

G♭

C♭

1 2 3 4 5 6 7

The Circle of Fifths

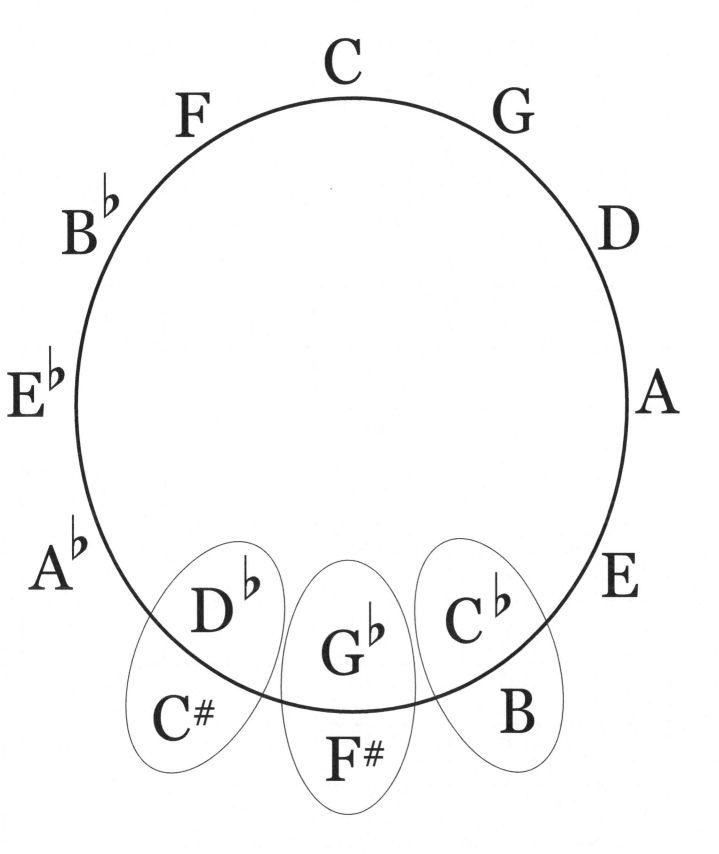

Spellings of All 15 Keys in Music

		Relative	Parallel
C	C D E F G A B C 1 2 3 4 5 6 7 1	A-	C-
G	G A B C D E F# G 1 2 3 4 5 6 7 1	E-	G-
D	D E F# G A B C# D 1 2 3 4 5 6 7 1	B-	D-
A	A B C# D E F# G# A 1 2 3 4 5 6 7 1	F#-	A-
E	E F# G# A B C# D# E 1 2 3 4 5 6 7 1	C#-	E-
B	B C# D# E F# G# A# B 1 2 3 4 5 6 7 1	G#-	B-
F#	F# G# A# B C# D# E# F# 1 2 3 4 5 6 7 1	D#-	F#-
C#	C# D# E# F# G# A# B# C# 1 2 3 4 5 6 7 1	A#-	C#-
C♭	C♭ D♭ E♭ F♭ G♭ A♭ B♭ C♭ 1 2 3 4 5 6 7 1	A♭-	C♭-
G♭	G♭ A♭ B♭ C♭ D♭ E♭ F G♭ 1 2 3 4 5 6 7 1	E♭-	G♭-
D♭	D♭ E♭ F G♭ A♭ B♭ C D♭ 1 2 3 4 5 6 7 1	B♭-	D♭-
A♭	A♭ B♭ C D♭ E♭ F G A♭ 1 2 3 4 5 6 7 1	F-	A♭-
E♭	E♭ F G A♭ B♭ C D E♭ 1 2 3 4 5 6 7 1	C-	E♭-
B♭	B♭ C D E♭ F G A B♭ 1 2 3 4 5 6 7 1	G-	B♭-
F	F G A B♭ C D E F 1 2 3 4 5 6 7 1	D-	F-

DO-IT-YOURSELF LEXICON

Define and explain the use of each term in a **SINGLE SENTENCE.**

Key –

Key Signature –

Pulse –

Tempo –

Meter –

Duration –

Rest –

Syncopation –

Rubato –

Dynamics –

Staccato –

Legato –

Accent –

Forte –

Piano –

Crescendo –

Diminuendo –

Interval –

Triad –

Seventh Chord –

Arpeggio –

Melody –

Harmony –

Counterpoint –

Chromatic –

Cadence –

Authentic Cadence -

Plagal Cadence -

Half Cadence -

Fermata -

Inversion -

Voicing -

Voice -

Tonality -

Tone -

Timbre -

Major -

Minor -

Soprano -

Alto -

Tenor -

Bass -

Augmented -

Augmentation -

Diminished -

Diminuition -

Harmonic Rhythm -

Diatonic -

Tonic -

Dominant -

Subdominant -

Relative Key-

Parallel Key -

Secondary Dominant -

Modulation -

Transposition –

Substitution –

Ostinato –

Phrase –

Phrasing –

Chord Tone –

Passing Tone –

Auxiliary tone –

Ornament –

Sequence –

Imitation –

Theme –

Variation –

Recapitulation –

Repeat –

Del Capo –

Del Segno –

Coda –

Verse –

Chorus –

Bridge –

A Section –

B Section –

Repeat –

Break –

Shot –

Progression –

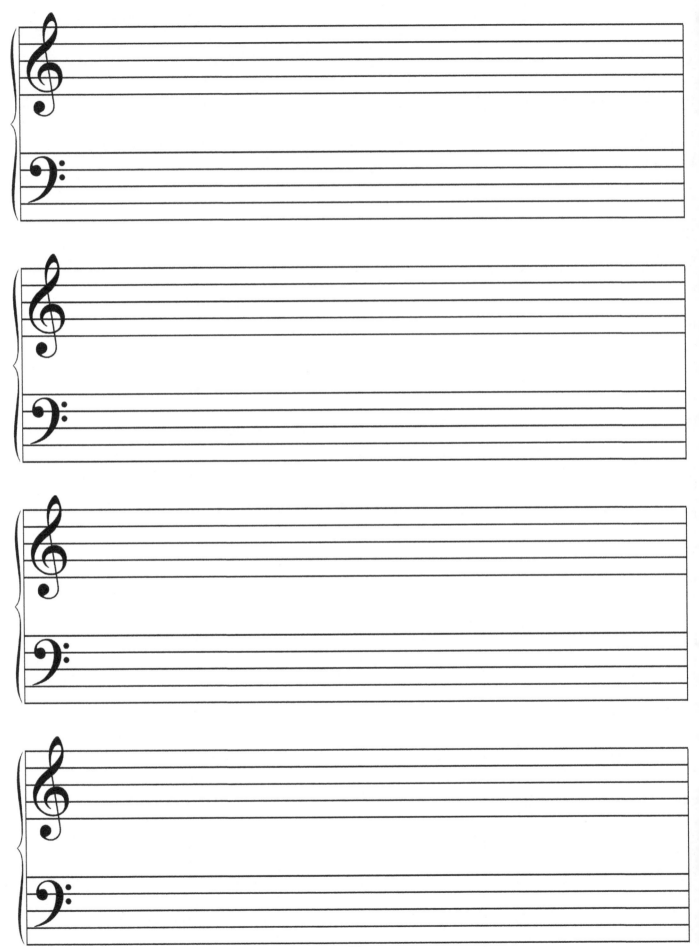

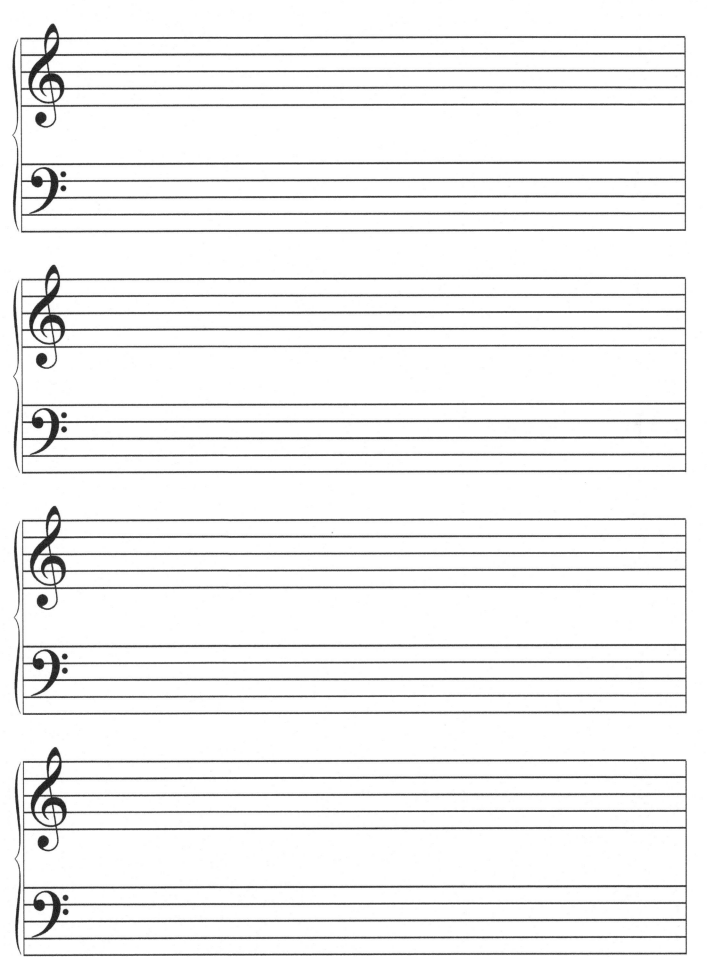

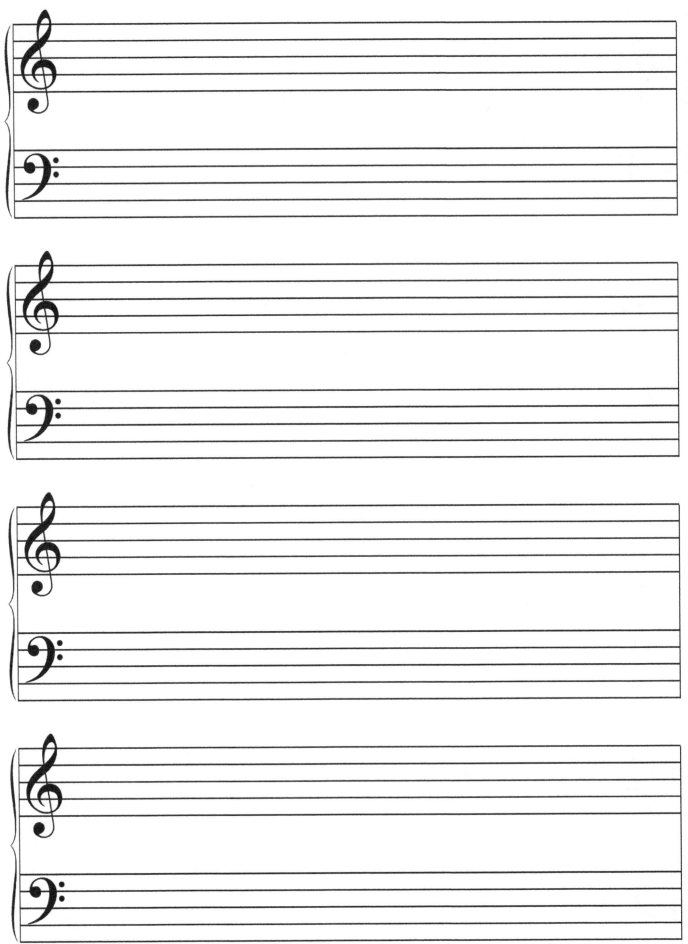

PUZZLE ANSWERS

Page 33

S	A	X	O	P	H	O	N	E		E	W
	Y		B	A	S	S	O	O	N		L	O
E		N					B			E	O
N	G		T	R	O	M	B	O	N	E	L	D
O	U		H	O			O			U	W
H	I		T	E		I	Z			K	I
P	T	L	T		S		A			U	N
O	A	A	U		S	S	I	K	M	U	R	D
L	R	L	U		A		Z				S
Y	F		C	L	A	R	I	N	E	T		S
X		R			B				R		A
	E			O	N	A	I	P			B
P	I	C	C	O	L	O	S	A	B	U	T

Page 33

Page 43

H	I	P	H	O	P	E	R	A	R	R		R
E	Y	G	O	S	P	E	L	A		O	K	H
A	A	U		R		P		R	C		Y
V	W		S	P	E		D		O	K	S	T
Y	D	P	E	O	G		I	R	C		S	H
M	A	O		B	G		S		K	C	A	M
E	O	W		E	A	R	C		A	L	R	A
T	R	O	P	B	E	A	O	Y	B	A	G	N
A	B	O		H		G	R	K	I	S	E	D
L	P	D	T		T		N	L	S	U	B
A	F	U	N	K	N	I		U	L	I	L	L
K	O	F	R	U	S	M		P	Y	C	B	U
S	L	S	O	U	L	E	N	E	W	A	G	E
	K	C	J	A	Z	Z		A	S	L	A	S

Page 43

Page 42

C Major Solid Triad

Whole Notes

C Major Broken Triad

Quarter Notes

D Major Solid Triad

Whole Notes

G Major Broken Triad

Quarter Notes

F Major Solid Triad

Half Notes

Unison C Major

5 Finger Pattern

Unison G Major

5 Finger Pattern

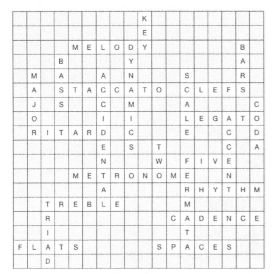

Page 47

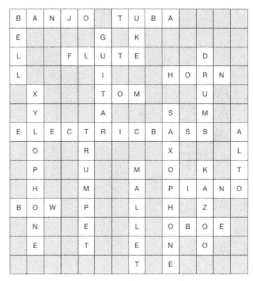

Page 53

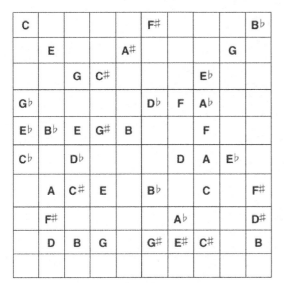

Page 56

Page 57

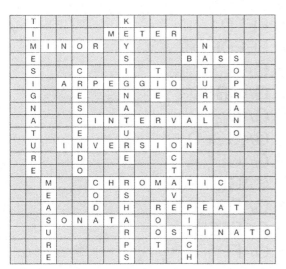

Page 61

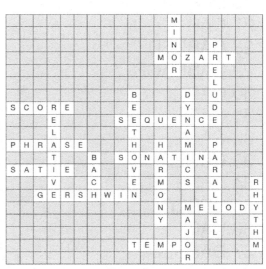

Page 85

1. AGE
2. AGED
3. ACE
4. ACED
5. ACCEDE
6. ACCEDED
7. ADAGE
8. ADD
9. ADDED
10. ADE
11. BABE
12. BAD
13. BADE
14. BADGE
15. BADGED
16. BAG
17. BAGGED
18. BAGGAGE
19. BED
20. BEDDED
21. BEAD
22. BEADED
23. BEG
24. BEGGED
25. BEEF
26. BEEFED
27. CAB
28. CABBED
29. CABBAGE
30. CAD
31. CAFE
32. CAGE
33. CAGED
34. CEDE
35. CEDED
36. DAB
37. DABBED
38. DAD

39. DEAF
40. DEAD
41. DECAF
42. DECADE
43. DEED
44. DEEDED
45. DEFACE
46. DEFACED
47. EBB
48. EBBED
49. EDGE
50. EDGED
51. EFFACE
52. EFFACED
53. EGG
54. EGGED
55. FAB
56. FACADE
57. FACE
58. FACED
59. FAD
60. FADE
61. FADED
62. FAG
63. FAGGED
64. FED
65. FEED
66. FEEDBAG
67. GAB
68. GABBED
69. GAG
70. GAGGED
71. GAGE
72. GAGED
73. GAFFE
74. GAFFED
75. GAFF

Key	MAJOR	MINOR
C	C E G	C E♭ G
G	G B D	G B♭ D
D	D F# A	D F A
A	A C# E	A C E
E	E G# B	E G B
B	B D# F#	B D F#
F#	F# A# C#	F# A C#
C#	C# E# G#	C# E G#
C♭	C♭ E♭ G♭	C♭ E♭♭ G♭
G♭	G♭ B♭ D♭	G♭ B♭♭ D♭
D♭	D♭ F A♭	D♭ F♭ A♭
A♭	A♭ C E♭	A♭ C♭ E♭
E♭	E♭ G B♭	E♭ G♭ B♭
B♭	B♭ D F	B♭ D♭ F
F	F A C	F A♭ C

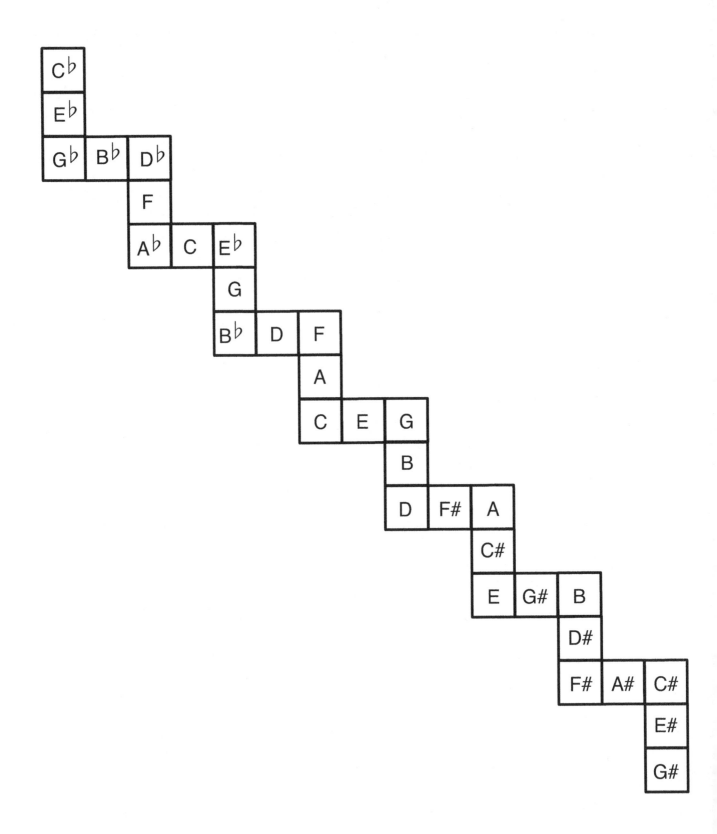

C	E	G
A♭	C	E♭
F	A	C

D♭	F	A♭
A	C#	E
G♭	B♭	D♭

D	F#	A
B♭	D	F
G	B	D

E♭	G	B♭
B	D#	F#
A♭	C	E♭

E	G#	B
C	E	G
A	C#	E

F	A	C
D♭	F	A♭
B♭	D	F

G♭	B♭	D♭
D	F#	A
B	D#	F#

G	B	D
E♭	G	B♭
C	E	G

A♭	C	E♭
E	G#	B
D♭	F	A♭

A	C#	E
F	A	C
D	F#	A

B♭	D	F
G♭	B♭	D♭
E♭	G	B♭

B	D#	F#
G	B	D
E	G#	B

C	E♭	G
A	C	E
F	A♭	C

D♭	F♭	A♭
B♭	D♭	F
G♭	B♭♭	D♭

D	F	A
B	D	F♯
G	B♭	D

E♭	G♭	B♭
C	E♭	G
A♭	C♭	E♭

E	G	B
C♯	E	G♯
A	C	E

F	A♭	C
D	F	A
B♭	D♭	F

G♭	B♭♭	D♭
E♭	G♭	B♭
B	D	F♯

G	B♭	D
E	G	B
C	E♭	G

A♭	C♭	E♭
F	A♭	C
D♭	F♭	A♭

A	C	E
F♯	A	C♯
D	F	A

B♭	D♭	F
G	B♭	D
E♭	G♭	B♭

B	D	F♯
A♭	C♭	E♭
E	G	B

Page 46

7

7

7

3

3

+ 12

_____

TOTAL: 39

Page 64

7

7

3

3

1

15

15

+ 12

_____

TOTAL: 63

MINOR	MAJOR	Accidentals
d	F	B♭
g	B♭	B♭ E♭
c	E♭	B♭ E♭ A♭
f	A♭	B♭ E♭ A♭ D♭
b♭	D♭	B♭ E♭ A♭ D♭ G♭
e♭	G♭	B♭ E♭ A♭ D♭ G♭ C♭
a♭	C♭	B♭ E♭ A♭ D♭ G♭ C♭ F♭
a	C	
e	G	F#
b	D	F# C#
f#	A	F# C# G#
c#	E	F# C# G# D#
g#	B	F# C# G# D# A#
d#	F#	F# C# G# D# A# E#
a#	C#	F# C# G# D# A# E# B#

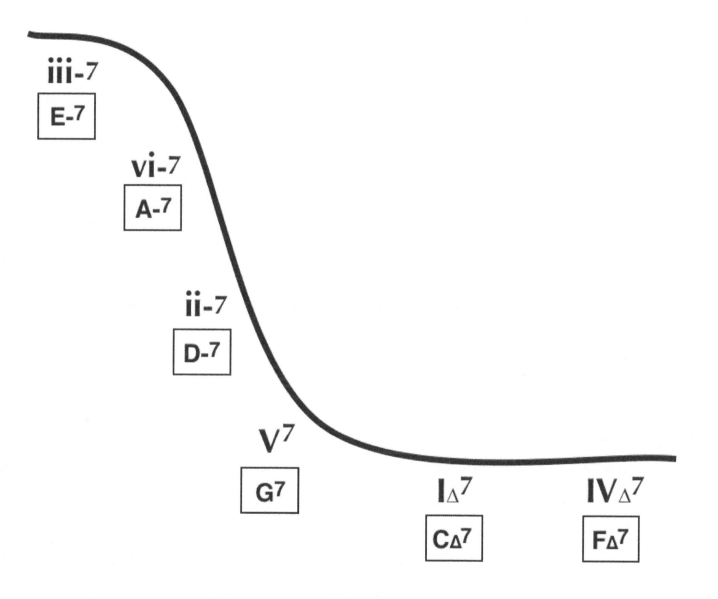

Key – A series of seven tones arranged in alpha-numerical order.

Key Signature – A group of sharps or flats displayed just to the right of the clef, indicating the key.

Pulse – Equidistant points on a temporal (time) line. Also referred to as the "beat".

Tempo – The rate of a pulse, measured in beats per minute (BPM).

Meter – The grouping of a pulse which results in a natural accent pattern.

Duration – The length of time a note is sounded.

Rest – A period of silence.

Syncopation – The interruption of the normal pattern of metrical accents in meter.

Rubato –The stretching and shrinking of note values within a pulse, for expression.

Dynamics – Varying and contrasting degrees of loudness or intensity.

Staccato – Notes sounding in a short, detached manner.

Legato – Notes sounding in a smooth, attached manner.

Accent – A note or notes sounded with greater emphasis than those around it, using dynamics or duration.

Forte – Loud.

Piano – Soft.

Crescendo – A directive to gradually increase the volume of the notes in a phrase or passage.

Diminuendo – A directive to gradually decrease the volume of the notes in a phrase or passage.

Interval – The measured distance between two pitches.

Triad – A three-note chord comprised of the Root, 3rd and 5th degrees of a scale.

Seventh Chord - A four-note chord comprised of the Root, 3rd, 5th and 7th degrees of a scale.

Arpeggio - The notes of a chord played one at a time in succession. Sometimes called a "Broken Chord".

Melody - A single note musical line, usually played in the soprano voice.

Harmony - Two or more notes sounded simultaneously, and also the study of chords in music.

Counterpoint - Two or more single note musical lines sounded simultaneously.

Chromatic – Scale consisting of all 12 semi-tones (half-steps) in the Western musical system.

Cadence - A moment of harmonic tension, followed by a moment of resolution.

Authentic Cadence - The V chord of a key resolving to the I chord of the same key.

Plagal Cadence - The IV chord of a key resolving to the I chord of the same key.

Half Cadence - The I chord of a key resolving temporarily to the V chord of the same key.

Fermata – A symbol used to indicate a long sustain of the note, the length of which is variable.

Inversion – Arranging of chord tones into a new shape, while keeping them as close together as possible.

Voicing – Arranging of chord tones into a new shape, in any intervallic order desired.

Voice – Name given to the individual notes of a chord, or single note lines within a harmonic progression.

Tonality – The relation of all the notes in a piece to one scale system built on a single tone.

Tone – An audible sound consisting of pitch, loudness, timbre and duration.

Timbre – The type of sound an instrument produces, determined by the prominence of specific overtones.

Major – One of the two basic tonalities in Western Music, considered the "brighter" tonality.

Minor – One of the two basic tonalities in Western Music, considered the "darker" tonality.

Soprano – Name given to the highest sounding note of a chord, or single note line in a piece of music.

Alto – Name given to the 2nd highest sounding note of a chord, or single note line in a piece of music.

Tenor – Name given to the 3rd highest sounding note of a chord, or single note line in a piece of music.

Bass – Name given to the lowest sounding note of a chord, or single note line in a piece of music.

Augmented – Term for a type of triad with a raised (sharped) 5th degree.

Augmentation – Rhythmic term for doubling the duration of notes within a phrase.

Diminished – Term for a type of triad with a lowered (flatted) 3rd and 5th degree.

Diminuition – Rhythmic term for halving the duration of notes within a phrase.

Harmonic Rhythm – The number beats, or measures that a chord change lasts.

Diatonic – Term given to describe the notes within a given key exclusively.

Tonic – Name given to the chord of a key built upon the first degree of a scale.

Dominant – Name given to the chord of a key built upon the 5th degree of a scale.

Subdominant – The chord of a key built upon the 4th degree of a scale.

Relative Key – A key having the same key signature as its major or minor counterpart.

Parallel Key – A key having the same tonic tone as its major or minor counterpart.

Secondary Dominant – A V chord borrowed from a key other than the initial key.

Modulation – The process of shifting from one tonality to another.

Transposition – The playing of a musical passage in a key other than the original.

Substitution – The practice of using one chord in place of another in a chord progression.

Ostinato – A repeating musical phrase or figure.

Phrase – A musical sentence; a complete musical thought.

Phrasing - The pace a performer sets in playing from phrase to phrase.

Chord Tone - A note in a melody which is one of the notes of the present chord.

Passing Tone - A non-chord tone in a melody, connecting two chord tones.

Auxiliary tone - A non-chord tone which moves a step from a chord tone.

Ornament - Compositional device using a series of tones surrounding the original.

Sequence - The re-statement of a phrase, a step higher or lower than the original.

Imitation - The re-statement of a phrase, at a different interval than the original.

Theme - A musical statement which serves as the basis for a composition.

Variation - A re-statement of the theme, with slight rhythmic or melodic changes.

Recapitulation - The re-statement of the main theme at the end of a section.

Del Capo - A directive to return to the very beginning of a piece of music.

Del Segno - A directive to return to a previous section of music, marked by a sign.

Coda - Symbol marking the exit and entry points that lead to the end of a piece.

Verse - Main section of a popular song, usually repeated multiple times.

Chorus - Section of a popular song which usually contains the title or the "hook".

Bridge - Section of a popular song which usually appears only once and introduces new chords.

A Section - Section of a song, usually the first half of a verse.

B Section - Section of a song, usually the second half of a verse. Sometimes called a "Pre-chorus".

Repeat - An enclosure symbol which indicates that everything within it should be played twice.

Break - An abrupt stop in the music, usually played in unison by all members of an ensemble.

Shot - An accent played in unison by all the members of an ensemble.

Progression - A term used to describe a group of chords played in succession.

Made in the USA
Monee, IL
16 August 2020

37636870R00066